Marco Lippi

NLB

Value and Naturalism in Marx

Translated by Hilary Steedman

First published as
Marx: il valore come costo sociale reale
by Etas Libri, Milan 1976
© Etas Libri S.p.A., 1976

This edition first published 1979
© NLB, 1979
NLB, 7 Carlisle Street, London W1

Typeset in English Times by
Red Lion Setters, London WC1

Printed and bound by CPI Group (UK) Ltd,
Croydon, CR0 4YY

ISBN 0 86091 018 0

Contents

Preface to the English Edition

In his *Theories of Value and Distribution since Adam Smith,* Maurice Dobb gives a short account of attempts to solve the so-called transformation problem, and classifies Sraffa's determination of prices and the rate of profit as a generalization of Bortkiewicz's traditional solution (see p. 161; although of course Dobb does not consider this the only significant contribution of Sraffa's *Production of Commodities by Means of Commodities).* Such an approach, in my opinion, loses sight of the real significance of Sraffa's work for Marx's theory of value, prices, and the rate of profit. Implicit in Sraffa's work is the proposition that prices and the rate of profit can be determined without ever considering values; the problem of transforming values into prices therefore no longer exists, at least in the way in which it was posed by Marx, as the *necessity* of determining prices through values.

It is of some importance to understand the reason for this sort of 'defensive' attitude towards Marx's theory of value. Why this evident attempt at 'reconciliation', especially on the part of an authority like Dobb, who stands poles apart from those Marxists whom Ian Steedman quite correctly termed 'the obscurants' in his *Marx after Sraffa*?

In other words, we must try to understand why Marxists have found it so difficult to come to terms with and fully develop results such as Sraffa's. Why has such great energy been expended defending Marx's theory as a body of thought in which no single element can be lost without jeopardizing the entire structure, when such an attitude has made it impossible to embark upon a positive reconstruction of economic theory based on Marx's premises?

The problem is not that Marxist tradition has strayed from the true meaning of Marx's thought. On the contrary, I would argue that Marx himself bears full responsibility for the tenacity with which 'orthodox' Marxists have defended his use of the labour theory of value. As I shall try to show in this book, the labour theory of value actually has a far wider significance than that of a simple analytical tool whose sole purpose is to determine prices and the rate of profit. For Marx, the identity of value and embodied labour follows from a general principle that transcends capitalist production; Marx's theory of value and prices then appears as an attempt to reduce this general principle to its application under a particular historical form of production. The task of science, Marx commented in his well-known letter to Kugelmann, is to explain how this general principle operates in the determination of exchange-values.

This notion that the 'task of science' requires that the characteristics of capitalism be explained on the basis of the labour theory of value became part of Marxist tradition with the work of Hilferding and has been consciously incorporated into some of the most significant work of Marxist economic theory, such as Paul Sweezy's *The Theory of Capitalist Development* and Dobb's *Political Economy and Capitalism*. It may also be found, although with less conscious intent, in the great majority of subsequent work on the transformation problem, in the attacks of the 'obscurants' on Sraffa, and in the call for greater depth of economic analysis in the context of the labour theory of value – even when such analysis, when not actually incorrect, amounts to an approach in which that theory no longer figures at all. (Several examples of such approaches are described in *Marx After Sraffa* and in chapter 4 of the present book as well.)

My purpose is to trace the whole question back to its origins. I examine how Marx came to identify value and labour, and how, as a result of this identification, strictly analytical objectives (the determination of prices and the rate of profit) were interwoven with a mass of pre-analytical observations about production in general. The exposition of these observations – which seem to me a 'naturalistic' element in Marx's reasoning about value (the idea being that a particular law of capitalism can be 'deduced' from a general law) – may perhaps encourage Marxists to assume a more critical attitude towards Marx himself. By this I mean that the theory of capitalism expounded in *Capital* can be separated from its formulation in terms of the labour theory of value. I have tried to show that this is possible (and I am certainly not the first to have done so) and that the adoption of a correct theory of prices and the rate of profit need not in itself invalidate Marx's propositions about exploitation, commodity fetishism, capitalist accumulation, and capitalist crisis, the truth or falsity of which does not depend on the labour theory of value.

In this English edition I have corrected a few errors in the Italian edition and have added a Postscript, taken from my contribution to a conference on Marx held in February 1978 at the University of Modena. I hope that this Postscript may help to clarify some aspects of the second chapter.

Modena, March 1979

Preface

The argumentation through which the principal thesis of this book is demonstrated consists in tracing a single idea that crops up in many places throughout Marx's work. This procedure requires detailed analysis of particular points that are often widely separated from one another, which entails the danger that the reader may lose the thread of the argument. Hence the rather elaborate introduction.

The book itself assumes familiarity both with the problems related to the formulation of the theory of prices by Marx and the classical economists and with recent controversy surrounding Sraffa and the consequences for Marx's theory of value of the conclusions presented in Pierro Sraffa's *Production of Commodities by Means of Commodities*. It should also be noted that my use of simple examples instead of more complex treatment – as in chapter 3 in the discussion of the idea that guided Marx in his determination of prices of production – was not inspired by any desire to approach these problems in an over-simplified manner. Rather it is my conviction that such problems can now be discussed without recourse to mathematical procedures out of all proportion to the objective; indeed, these frequently succeed only in confusing the issue.

I am indebted to many people for criticisms, suggestions, and help of all kinds: Giovanni Ciccotti, Andrea Jovane, Adriana Lippi, Maria Cristina Marcuzzo, Bruno Miconi, Umberto Mosco, Valentina Ottolini, Gianfranco Pala, Paola Potestio, Giorgio Rodano, Salvatore Veca, and all my friends of the Facoltà di Economia e Commercio at Modena University. This work originated during a period of close collaboration with Bruna Ingrao, to whom my warmest thanks are due.

Modena, June 1976

Introduction

The first volume of *Capital* opens with the problem of exchange-value. When commodities are exchanged, Marx argues, certain quantities of different use-values are posited as equal. This implies, he continues, that the different commodities have some common element that is reflected in this equality. 'This common element', he writes, 'cannot be a geometrical, physical, chemical, or other natural property of commodities. Such properties come into consideration only to the extent that they make the commodities useful, i.e. turn them into use-values'.[1] Once the use-values of commodities are excluded, 'only one property remains, that of being products of labour'.[2] Human labour is therefore the 'substance' of value, and the quantities of labour required to produce the various commodities determine the magnitude of their values.

This 'deduction' is highly problematic, whether considered in isolation or in the light of the further development of the theory of value in the three volumes of *Capital*. Let us first consider this second point, the relationship between the quantitative determination of value as embodied labour and the empirical manifestation of exchange, which seems to have been Marx's point of departure. We know for certain that Marx does not maintain that commodities are actually exchanged according to the quantities of labour embodied in them, as may be seen, to give but one example, from an explicit statement to the contrary, again in the first volume of *Capital*: in note 24 of chapter 5. Here Marx distinguishes between *average price* and *market price*. The former, which is the point

---

[1] Marx, *Capital* Volume 1, Penguin Books in association with New Left Review, Harmondsworth, 1976, p. 127.
[2] Ibid., p. 128.

around which the latter fluctuates, is determined by value, but only in the final analysis: 'average prices do not directly coincide with the values of commodities, as Adam Smith, Ricardo, and others believe'.[3] Here Marx is anticipating the problem of the difference between value and price of production, which is dealt with in the third volume of *Capital*, where he criticizes Smith and Ricardo for having directly determined actual exchange rates from quantities of embodied labour.[4]

The concept of value arises from the problem of exchange, but is then related to it through a twofold mediation. First, values are directly linked to average prices and not to market prices (which are immediately observable magnitudes);[5] second, however, values govern average prices only 'in the final analysis' and are not identical to them. Thus, starting from the problem of exchange, Marx 'deduces' a concept and a magnitude of value that do not directly account for exchange. On the other hand, he never presents value as a secondary concept or mere definition, nor an analytical tool used merely as a provisional basis for the theoretical determination of observable magnitudes (and the relationships between them): prices of production, the rate of profit (the relation between the latter and the wage-rate). Nor is value ever justified as a first approximation, as has sometimes been done in the tradition that claims allegiance to Marx.

But this is not all. Marx refines and develops the concept of value so as to confirm and deepen its autonomy. The analysis of pure costs of circulation in *Capital* Volume 2 and the exclusion of these costs from value formation is developed independently of, indeed in direct contrast to, the formation of actual exchange-values. In Marx's treatment of the value of agricultural products we find the same contrast between *real* costs and what *appears* in prices as a

[3] Ibid., p. 269.

[4] This point will be discussed more fully below.

[5] The object of both Marx's and the classical economists' theory of exchange-value is always the average around which market prices fluctuate. These magnitudes are also described by Marx as the averages of market prices over time. As we shall see, Marx holds that these average magnitudes – the prices of production – can be determined only on the basis of an ultimate magnitude: value. In Volume 1, Marx refers to the exchange-value of one commodity in terms of another as the ratio of the quantities of labour embodied in them. But this is not an actual exchange-value, as we have seen. Later we shall examine in detail the use of this magnitude in the first two volumes of *Capital*.

result of competition. The 'real price of production' is the *average* necessary labour and not the 'false social value' represented by the labour required on ground less fertile than average.

In the course of this work we shall discuss at length these and other conspicuous signs of a 'theory of production in general' in Marx's work.[6] We shall argue that it is here that the reasons why Marx identified magnitude of value with quantity of embodied labour must be sought. Indeed, in a well-known and frequently quoted passage from a letter to Kugelmann, Marx characterized the concept of value as a 'law of nature' and defined the task of science as the investigation of the *forms* in which the law operates![7] The development of the thesis of the identity of value and labour, together with this explicit formulation of it, will form the basis of our attempt to reconstruct the foundation of Marx's theory of value. This reconstruction may be summarized as follows.

The measurement of products by the quantity of labour necessary to produce them and the distribution of social labour among the various activities required to meet various needs (in accordance with that measure) are general characteristics of human social life. Labour, as a measure of difficulties that must be overcome, as *real social cost*,[8] is the 'immanent measure' of the product, whatever the

[6] Exactly what I mean by 'production in general' will be clarified below, particularly in chapter 2.

[7] Letter to Kugelmann, 11 July 1868, in Marx-Engels, *Selected Works*, volume 2, Moscow, 1962, p. 461.

[8] In *Capital* Volume 3, Marx uses the terms 'wirkliche Kost' (real cost) and 'wirkliche Wert' (real value) to contrast the quantity of embodied labour with 'Kostpreis' (the sum of constant and variable capital, which he also calls 'kapitalistische Kost') and 'Produktionspreis' (the price obtained after transformation) respectively. He also uses the term 'wirklicher Produktionspreis' (real production price) to make a similar distinction between the average price of the agricultural product of lands of differing levels of fertility and the price of production on less fertile land, for which he uses the term 'falscher sozialer Wert' ('false social value'). In the English translation from which the quotations are taken here (*Capital* Volume 3, Lawrence and Wishart, London, 1974), the term 'wirklich' is translated as 'actual' in the first and third instances (p. 26, p. 661) and 'real' in the second (p. 175). It is important, however, to emphasize the common element in these distinctions – which Marx expresses by using the same term, 'wirklich' – between socially necessary embodied labour and the various other magnitudes that replace it in the phenomenology of exchange and/or in the consciousness of the participants in production and distribution. 'Principle of real cost' refers to the idea – present in Smith and Ricardo and central in Marx, as we shall see – that the labour required to produce objects is *a measure of those objects as products*, independent of their existence as objects of exchange. We shall therefore use the term 'real social cost' in order to emphasize the socially objective character Marx attributes to the magnitude of embodied labour, as opposed to Smith's concept of labour as sacrifice.

historical mode of production. Marx develops this principle of real cost as a framework for the reconstruction on the basis of labour of every phenomenon related to commodities and exchange-value. Value is merely the *form* assumed by real cost when the objects in question are commodities, products to be exchanged. The magnitude of value is precisely the real cost; hence Marx's very sharp distinction between circulation costs and production costs in the strict sense; hence also his approach to the value of agricultural products. Values are such costs inasmuch as they have become entities estranged from the producers; they are privately executed labour which appears to the producers as an objective quality of things; this second aspect of value is developed in the notion of abstract labour, and in the theory of fetishism.

But let us come to the crucial point in Marx's investigation. What is the connection between value and actual exchange-value? The basis of the exchange of commodities is the quantity of labour expended in their production. Actual exchange-values do not reflect such magnitudes directly, since the picture is complicated by the need for uniform distribution of profit among capitalists, by rent, and by *faux frais*. But that which can be shared out in the various forms of income, together with that which reconstitutes used up means of production, is measured exactly by the labour expended in production and embodied in the total product. Prices merely redistribute surplus-value among industrial capitalists, merchants, and landowners.[9]

We shall see that Marx's theory of the determination of prices – which is not confined to the well-known pages on the transformation problem in Part II of *Capital* Volume 3, since it is also involved in the discussion of commercial capital and rent – is ever dominated by this premise. For Marx, the conservation of total quantities of value and surplus-value is the way the 'law of nature' asserts itself under commodity production. Behind the facade of prices, Marx held, labour is the only real cost; even more important, profit is nothing but the superficial manifestation of surplus-value, and therefore of surplus labour. In other words, the aim of Marx's approach is to reduce to embodied labour various magnitudes that are generally not

---

[9] This introduction and chapters 1 and 2 refer in general terms to the idea of the redistribution of surplus-value. In chapter 3 it will be examined in more detail.

proportional to quantities of embodied labour. This reduction cannot be arbitrary, but must be consistent with the distinction between the *production* of value and surplus-value and a (logically) subsequent *redistribution* of surplus-value among capitalists and between capitalists and landowners.[10] But there is only one legitimate way to make this distinction between the production and distribution of value and surplus-value: it must be argued that prices can be derived from values by means of the transfer from some commodities to others of part of the labour expended in total production. The conservation of the total quantities of labour expended, far from being an expedient of minor importance (as many have tended to believe), occupies a central role in Marx's theoretical construction.

In chapter 5 of the *Wealth of Nations*, Adam Smith makes a distinction between labour as 'the real price of every thing, that which every thing costs for him who needs to obtain it for himself', and the nominal price – the price in money terms – of commodities. He starts with a general definition of wealth and a hypothetical comparison between the production of commodities – which Smith does not distinguish from the division of labour – and a situation in which each person produces what he needs for himself. Smith writes: 'Every man is rich or poor according to the degree in which he can afford to enjoy the necessaries, conveniences, and amusements of human life. But after the division of labour has once thoroughly taken place, it is but a very small part of these with which a man's own labour can supply him.' The real valuation of things as exchange-values arises from this comparison: 'The real price of every thing . . . is the toil and trouble of acquiring it'. Whoever owns a commodity will, when exchanging it, value it in terms of 'the toil and trouble which it can save to himself, and which it can impose upon other people'. Thus the 'money' or 'goods' that we exchange for other goods 'contain the value of an equal quantity'.[11]

This measure of the difficulties encountered in production – 'At all times and places that is dear which it is difficult to come at, or which it costs much labour to acquire; and that cheap which is to be

---

[10] The entire structure of the argument of *Capital* is based on this distinction.

[11] Adam Smith, *An Inquiry into the Nature and Causes of the Wealth of Nations*, New York, 1937, p. 30.

had easily or with very little labour'[12] – determines exchange-value until capital has been accumulated and land appropriated.[13] When commodities are produced under capitalism, prices are the outcome of the 'addition'[14] of wages, profit, and rent. These components are determined, independent of one another, by the conjunction of the supply and demand for labour, capital, and land respectively. Variations of price correspond to quantitatively equivalent variations in wage levels, profits, and rents.

In his *On the Principles of Political Economy and Taxation,* David Ricardo accepts Smith's assertion that labour is the real price and 'original source of exchange value'.[15] On this basis he reveals the error of the theory that prices are determined by a process of 'addition'. The division of the product between profits and wages does not in itself cause prices to change. Ricardo showed that under certain hypothetical conditions commodities would be exchanged in accordance with the quantities of embodied labour whatever the division of the product between profits and wages. Under these hypotheses, the central proposition of Ricardo's system could easily be proven: an increase in wages results in a fall in the rate of profit and not in an increase in prices. However, once he had admitted different proportions between fixed and circulating capital and different turnover times – that is, once these particular hypothetical conditions had been withdrawn – Ricardo encountered difficulties because of modifications, caused by these differences, of the principle that exchange-value is regulated by quantities of embodied labour.[16] Ricardo never overcame these difficulties, and was therefore unable properly to prove his central proposition that the rate of profit varies with changes in wage levels. But he never abandoned the idea that labour was the real cost and principal cause of exchange-value, the other factors merely producing modifications.

---

[12] Ibid., p. 33.

[13] Ibid., p. 47

[14] For Marx's description of Smith's theory of price as an 'addition' of separate elements see *Theories of Surplus Value*, London, 1969, Volume II, p. 217. See also Sraffa, 'Introduction' to D. Ricardo, *On the Principles of Political Economy and Taxation*, in Ricardo, *Works and Correspondence*, London 1951, Volume I, pp.xiii-lxiii.

[15] Ricardo, ibid., pp. 12-13.

[16] Ricardo speaks of modifications in sections IV and V of the chapter 'On Value' in his *Principles*.

Indeed, Ricardo himself came to develop a distinction between 'positive value' and 'exchange-value': 'I do not . . . say that the labour expended on a commodity is a measure of its exchangeable value, but of its positive value. . . . You say that if there were no exchange of commodities they could have no value, and I agree with you if you mean exchangeable value, but if I am obliged to devote one month's labour to make me a coat, and only one week's labour to make a hat, although I should never exchange either of them, the coat would be four times the value of the hat'.[17] (Here value is explicitly identified with labour on the basis of considerations both extraneous and prior to the problem of exchange-value.)

And again, in his last work: 'I may be asked what I mean by the word value, and by what criterion I would judge whether a commodity had or had not changed its value. I answer, I know no other criterion of a thing being dear or cheap but by the sacrifices of labour – nothing that has value can be produced without it.'[18]

Marx reformulated all these themes in the following ways. In the first place, he distinguished between value and price more precisely and emphatically. He held that prices of production differed from values and criticized Ricardo for not having distinguished them with sufficient clarity. Second, Marx freed labour as real cost from the subjective element it had in Smith (labour as positive activity as opposed to labour as sacrifice).[19] Third, Marx sharply demarcated labour from the *faux frais* that originate from the commodity form as such (like pure costs of circulation). Furthermore, he counterposed the socio-historical characteristics of commodity-producing labour to those of labour in general.

Value thus emerges as a mixed category. On the one hand, its magnitude is determined on the basis of the consideration of production in general, independent of the historical context of such production; it has a natural social basis, like Smith's and Ricardo's principle of real price. On the other hand, it is the form such a magnitude assumes when the products of labour are commodities;

[17] Letter to Hutches Trower, 4 July 1821, in *Works and Correspondence of David Ricardo*, London, 1952, Volume IX, p. 2.

[18] 'Absolute Value and Exchangeable Value', in *Works and Correspondence,* Volume IV, p. 397. We shall return to these aspects of Ricardo's thought in Chapter 4.

[19] In chapter 2 we will deal with Marx's analysis of these passages of *The Wealth of Nations*.

Smith and Ricardo, Marx holds, understood the magnitude of value but never analysed its form.[20]

The first three chapters of this book are devoted to developing the themes we have touched on so far. The fourth chapter (and part of the second) concerns the analysis of recent arguments about Marx's theory of value, which has been the subject of major developments since the beginning of the 1960s.[21] Great progress has undoubtedly been made. The relationship between amounts of embodied labour and prices of production has been completely clarified. At the same time, another line of research has uncovered the specific historical characteristics of abstract labour, which Marx held to constitute the substance of value.[22] But the central question seems to have been avoided. It is one thing to ask what exactly is this labour that Marx identifies with value and what is the relationship between magnitudes of embodied labour, prices of production, and profits. It is quite a different matter – and here analysis is lacking – to ask *why* Marx identified value with embodied labour and whether such an identification retains any meaning, apart from that of mere definition, in the light of the results achieved by the theory of prices of production. This is the central theme of this book. I shall try to

[20] See the famous passage on 'political economy' in section 4 of chapter 1, *Capital* Volume 1, 'The Fetishism of Commodities and its Secret', which will be extensively quoted in chapter 2 of this book. Marx uses the term 'form' when speaking of the way certain determinants of production in general appear under capitalist production; in particular, value is the form assumed by cost in labour when products are commodities. The same term, 'form', is used for all manifestations of value: exchange-value, money, price etc. Profit too is the 'form' surplus-value assumes in appearance. (Marx calls profit the 'transformed form' (*verwandelte Form*) of surplus-value; also, to emphasize the emergence of profit generated from advances of capital, he calls it the 'mystified form' (*mystifizierte Form*) of surplus-value; see *Capital* Volume 3, London, 1974, p. 36.) There is a superimposition of forms as we move from the form of value assumed by labour when it is producing commodities to that which is immediately observable. Smith and Ricardo penetrated the surface forms – wherein lies their achievement – and thereby arrived at value. But they failed to understand that value is only a form assumed by labour; in other words, since they did not distinguish with sufficient clarity between commodity production and production in general, they presented the form assumed by labour in value as eternal. These points will be discussed at greater length in the final chapter.

[21] Since, that is, the publication of Sraffa's work in 1960 and of Garegnani's in the same year. We owe to these authors the complete and definitive solution of the problem of prices in the theory of Marx and of the classical economists.

[22] I am referring here mainly to the work of Lucio Colletti, which will be discussed at length later.

show that Marx's theory of value is dominated in all its aspects by a 'naturalistic' element that must be eliminated, since it leads to incorrect results. On the other hand – and this is another aim of the book – it will be shown that the central propositions of *Capital* retain their meaning despite their formulation in terms of the labour theory of value and that their validity does not depend on the validity of that theory.

Nevertheless, rejection of the labour theory of value does entail an important shift in viewpoint, which we shall attempt to define in our conclusions.

Before the points outlined here are developed, however, one additional preliminary clarification is required, in order to minimize irritating repetition (minimize, but not eliminate entirely, for Marx's reasoning is highly intricate at times). We have said that Marx in no way claims that labour-values represent actual exchange-values. Our purpose in making this point was to emphasize the autonomous basis of Marx's concept of value. At the same time, however, Marx does *also* use value as the equivalent of actual exchange-value. Values and market prices occupy antipodal 'ontological ranks' in the structure of Marx's theory. They are linked by a chain of mediations, as follows. Market prices fluctuate around magnitudes which Marx calls average prices. The latter are the prices of production, which guarantee equal rates of profit in all industries. Prices of production, on the other hand, exist only as modified values and can therefore be ascertained only on the basis of values. Hence, in order to understand fluctuations of market prices, the scientific economist must re-trace the whole chain that begins with value. It is important to stress this point: in Marx's theory, prices of production, while they are considerably more 'real' than market prices, cannot even be conceived except as transformed values. Since production prices are only a manifestation of those 'ultimate' exchange-values determined by the ratio of quantities of embodied labour, the intervention of production prices is often disregarded and the relationships between quantities of embodied labour treated as though they were identical to average prices. An important example of this is the note to the fifth chapter of *Capital* Volume 1 cited above. What really interests Marx in this passage is the formal distinction between average price and market price as a means of eliminating consideration of random profits and losses. He works with average price as though it were identical to value, and only at the end of the discussion does he note that in fact there is a difference between them, value regulating average price only in the final analysis. The same method is employed in chapter 10 of *Capital* Volume 3, at the heart of the discussion of the transformation of values into prices of production. A lengthy analysis is devoted to the concept of market-value (which we shall consider in our first chapter), market price (which revolves around market-value), and the fluctuations of supply and demand (which determine the ups and downs of market prices). Only at the end of the chapter does Marx state that 'everything concerning' the market-value 'applies with appropriate modifications to the price of production'.[23] He then posits a 'market price of production' alongside the concept of market-value.

There are two additional reasons why Marx used value instead of prices of production in dealing with actual exchange-value. First, he considered the former a good substitute for the latter in dealing with variations caused by changes in methods of production (Ricardo was convinced of this too). It is this that justifies the use of value throughout the portion of Volume 1 devoted to the study of the 'laws of motion' of capitalist society. Second, because of the conservation of total quantities of embodied labour associated with the transformation of values into prices, the difference between values and prices has no effect on the study of aggregate magnitudes.[24]

[23] *Capital* Volume 3, p. 198.

[24] There seems to be no basis for the idea upheld by Sweezy in his *Theory of Capitalist Development* that in the first two volumes of *Capital* Marx is reasoning on the basis of the hypothesis that the organic composition of capital in the various branches of industry is identical, which would ensure the uniformity of the rate of profit, with prices proportionate to values. On the contrary, differences in organic compositions and concentration of attention on aggregate magnitudes are implicit in the following passage from the beginning of chapter 25 of *Capital* Volume 1, pp. 762-3: 'the average of all the average compositions in all branches of production gives us the composition of the total social capital of a country, and it is with this alone that we are concerned here in the final analysis'.

I

Productive Labour and Pure Circulation Costs

1. Marx: Value and Commercial Capital

In *Capital* Volume 1, after describing the changes in the organization of labour in the factories associated with the transformation of capitalism up to the period of manufacture, Marx returns to the concept of productive labour, which he had introduced in chapter 5 in connection with his analysis of the labour process. When this process becomes cooperative, Marx argues, important changes result: 'In order to work productively, it is no longer necessary for the individual to put his hand to the object; it is sufficient for him to be an organ of the collective labourer, and to perform any one of its subordinate functions.'[1] It is therefore to the collective labourer that one must refer in considering the labour embodied in a particular commodity. Under these conditions, unlike when 'the labour process is purely individual',[2] we must include in the calculation of embodied labour those workers who perform tasks not directly connected to the material transformation of the object of labour (ensuring the correct co-ordination between the different parts of the collective labourer is an example of this.)

The concept of productive labour is thus broadened beyond its earlier definition (in chapter 5, where it was linked to the individual labour process). At the same time, once the labour process is viewed no longer merely as a relationship between man and nature, but in the historical form it assumes under capitalism, 'the concept of productive labour also becomes narrower', for now in order to be a

---

[1] *Capital* Volume 1, pp. 643-44.
[2] Ibid., p. 643.

productive worker 'it is no longer sufficient . . . simply to produce'; it is necessary to produce surplus-value. In other words, the only productive workers are those whose labour 'contributes towards the self-valorization of capital'.[3]

It should be noted that Marx saw the second concept of productive labour as a *restriction* of the first. If a worker is to be productive in the capitalist sense (that is, productive of surplus-value), he must also be productive in the first sense – that is, part of the collective labourer as defined on the basis of the labour process and therefore productive of value. This point is not at all trivial since, as we shall soon see, Marx held that some wage workers employed within the circuit of capital do not produce even value, let alone surplus-value. (The concept of productive labour is of concern to us here only as it relates to Marx's theory of value. We shall therefore concentrate on the first distinction between productive and unproductive labour and shall not consider the complications arising from the existence of workers who may be paid wages but are employed outside the circuit of capital.)

In *Capital* Volume 2, when Marx analyses the process of circulation of commodities, and in Volume 3, when he deals with commercial profit, the problem arises of the workers whose labour is required for buying and selling, book-keeping, and the storage and transport of commodities. Intimately related to this is the question of the costs in materials and fixed capital consequent to these operations. In discussing these types of labour and costs, Marx asks whether they should be considered components of the value of commodities. He answers that all those costs that are strictly necessary under given technological conditions for the production, storage, and transport of the commodity as a particular physical product must be included. On the other hand, the *pure circulation costs* – those which 'arise due to the product having the economic form of a commodity'[4] – must be excluded. Also excluded are book-keeping costs that represent necessary expenditure regardless of the form of the product as a commodity.[5] This distinction is quite

[3] Ibid., p. 644.

[4] *Capital* Volume 3, London, 1974, p. 289.

[5] For book-keeping costs see *Capital* Volume 2, pp. 211-213 (Penguin/NLR edition). Transport costs are of course included in the value of the commodity (pp. 225-229), while as far as the maintenance of stocks is concerned, Marx includes only those costs

important. In fact, as we shall see shortly, Marx's careful separation of costs that contribute to the value of goods and those that do not does not necessarily correspond to an analogous distinction made by the agents of capitalist production and circulation, as Marx himself was well aware. The concept of value, however, as is now becoming clear, is not intended to account for phenomena directly. On the contrary, implicit in the definition of the magnitude of value that flows from the exclusion of circulation costs is the notion of a conflict between a capitalist manner and a *real* manner of viewing costs. Prices do not mirror values directly, although, as we shall see, they can and must be reconstructed on the basis of values.

Let us now look more closely at the question of circulation costs. In chapter 6 of *Capital* Volume 2 Marx discusses the operations of buying, selling and book-keeping. When the products of labour are commodities, a portion of total social labour-power must be devoted to such operations. But so long as they are carried out by the producers themselves, these producers know that the time taken up by them is deducted from time left over after production; there is no reason to confuse time required for production with time required for buying and selling. When production and circulation are dominated by capital, however, the operations required for circulation become autonomous, either within the productive unit or through their exclusive assumption by commercial capital. Then, Marx argues, the simple picture of pure circulation costs as deductions disappears as the result of this autonomy: 'An illusion is introduced here by the function of merchant's capital.'[6]

In actual fact, the costs incurred by commercial capitalists (wages paid to shop assistants, book-keepers, etc. and the cost of the materials required for these operations), appear in prices on the same footing as strictly productive costs. But even apart from

strictly necessary to guarantee continuity of production and consumption, regardless of the commodity-form assumed by the product. He treats labour associated with supervision and co-ordination in the same manner. In so far as this is a task arising from the division of labour, it is productive activity. However, since this function also arises as a result of the antagonistic character of the capitalist mode of production, it can be assimilated to labour expended in pure circulation. (See *Capital* Volume 1, pp. 443-44 and *Theories of Surplus-Value*, London, 1969, p. 505.) In this last-mentioned case, the difficulty of drawing a line of demarcation between the productive and unproductive aspects of the same function emerges with particular clarity.

[6] *Capital* Volume 2, p.209.

commercial capital, the pure circulation costs incurred by industrial capitalists are distinguished from other costs only if they are abnormal for a given industry.[7] Thus, a superficial glance at the entire process of production and distribution would suggest that all workers employed within the circuit of capital are equally productive. This interweaving and superimposition of distribution and production costs does not affect Marx's definition of the magnitude of value: 'The division of labour, with one function becoming independent in this way, does not make this into a product- or value-forming function if it is not so in itself, and thus was already so before it became independent.'[8] Only those functions that 'contribute to making the product' in the wider sense discussed above 'contribute to creating value', regardless of how things may seem from the formation of prices.

The formation of prices must therefore be clearly distinguished from the formation of values. The fact that the employee of a commercial capitalist may receive a wage which is then transferred to the price of the commodity has nothing to do with the magnitude of the value of that commodity, but involves only the distribution of total surplus-value. Marx's idea can be summarized quite simply as follows.[9]

For the sake of convenience, let us assume that all the operations required for circulation are performed entirely by commercial capitalists. The value of total output is measured by the total *productive labour* necessary to obtain it. Total value may be divided into three parts: C, the value of the means of production consumed; V, the value of the total labour-power employed; and S, the surplus-value, which is the difference between the labour added to the means of production and the magnitude V. The wages of the unproductive workers, the reconstitution of the 'constant capital' employed in distribution, and the profit appropriated by the commercial capitalists are deductions from the surplus-value extracted from productive workers by the industrial capitalists. This transfer of surplus-value is the origin of the 'increase' of prices that occurs when commodities are handled by commercial capital. But such an

[7] We shall return to Marx's views on this later.
[8] *Capital* Volume 2, p.212.
[9] Here we are anticipating a point that will be examined in chapter 3, in our discussion of price formation.

increase is possible only inasmuch as the industrial capitalists do not appropriate all the surplus-value *produced*; it is therefore counterbalanced by a deduction in the productive sector: 'Just as industrial capital makes profit by selling labour embodied and realized in commodities, for which it has not paid any equivalent, so merchant's capital derives profit from not paying in full to productive capital for all the unpaid labour contained in the commodities (in commodities, in so far as capital invested in their production functions as an aliquot part of the total industrial capital), and by demanding payment for this unpaid portion still contained in the commodities when making a sale.'[10] Now, if we further simplify matters by assuming that commercial capitalists are involved only in the buying and selling of consumer goods and that no expenditure of any sort by industrial capitalists is required for sales among themselves, then it follows that a commodity is sold at its value by the commercial capitalist by virtue of the fact that it is acquired at a price less than its value. We therefore have a distinction between the formation of prices and the formation of values and a reconstruction of the former on the basis of the latter.

When we examine Marx's view of the formation of prices, we shall return to this conception of commercial profits and this reconstitution of pure circulation costs. We shall find that Marx's procedure, however divergent it may appear from the way in which prices are actually formed, encounters no greater difficulties than the notion that prices of production are formed through the redistribution of surplus-value. For the moment, let us comment on what we have set out so far.

Every time Marx deals with pure circulation costs he resorts to a line of argumentation based on the contrast between a situation in which the operations required for circulation have become autonomous and thus appear on the same footing as those required for production (and are therefore confused with them) and a situation during the 'period' when such operations were still the direct province of the producers.[11] The exclusion of these costs from

---

[10] *Capital*, Volume 3, p.293.

[11] For this see *Capital*, Volume 2, pp. 289-290. Marx also deals with this problem at length in the *Grundrisse* (Penguin Books in association with New Left Review, Harmondsworth, 1973). For the line of argument under discussion here, see p. 624.

value invariably follows. Now, the 'period' to which Marx refers, when there was a clear separation between the processes of production and of pure circulation, has a twofold significance, as so often in Marx; it is both an abstraction and a particular historical observation.[12] Of these two meanings, the first is more important. Indeed, to arrive at the concept of value requires that all the costs incurred by industrial and commercial capitalists be sorted out and a precise distinction made between those connected with pure circulation and those connected with production. In other words, the material skeleton of the production process must be distinguished from the process as a whole; the greater the weight of pure costs of circulation as capitalism develops, and the more inextricable the inter-relationship between production in the strict sense and the commodity form of the product becomes, the more difficult it becomes to make that distinction.[13]

But what is most interesting about Marx's handling of pure circulation costs is that the distinction among costs associated with that abstraction is not designed simply to establish a classification that can set these out in order of their importance and demonstrate which costs could be eliminated or reduced if production were organized differently.[14] There is much more: the distinction affects the magnitude of value, and this magnitude is *objective* in character. Observable magnitudes are directly derived from value: the prices of commodities and the rate of profit are obtained beginning with the magnitudes of value, through the redistribution of surplus-value between industrial and commercial capitalists. A model of Marx's theory of value is thus inherent in his treatment of circulation costs. On the one hand, the principle of real cost is driven to its ultimate conclusions, through a logic extraneous and counterposed to that which dominates the formation of actual exchange-values; but on the other hand, this deepening of the concept of real cost does not

[12] See *Capital* Volume 2, p. 211, where he mentions, among other things, book-keeping during the Middle Ages.

[13] On this point, see P. Santi and M. Salvati, 'Critiche ortodosse a Sweezy e Baran', in *Problemi del Socialismo*, no. 34, 1968. The examples presented by Marx can be handled very simply.

[14] At the very most, Marx holds that pure circulation costs could be avoided if production were consciously organized. The exception is book-keeping costs, which are necessary whether products are commodities or not, but even these would diminish if the capitalist system were abolished. (See *Capital* Volume 2, pp. 211-212.)

loosen the bond between embodied labour and real exchange-values, but only lengthens the chain of mediations required to obtain the latter from the former.

2.   Marx and the Classical Economists

Among the passages Marx devoted to pure circulation costs and commercial capital we find two references to Ricardo. He cites a note in the *Principles* in which Ricardo expresses disagreement with Say's view that commercial transactions add value to goods in a manner no different from usual: 'Because more labour has been expended in its production and transport'.[15] Ricardo's thesis is the same as Marx's: the labour expended in transport and the consequent consumption of means of transport must be considered as added to the value of commodities. Similar considerations apply to the shift of location of objects in the course of each production process. Ricardo, then, unlike Say, does not make the mistake of attributing miraculous value-creating capacities to commercial transactions. On the other hand, Ricardo identifies commercial transactions with transport and mentions no other costs incurred by commercial capitalists. In the first chapter of the *Principles*, he speaks of 'the labour of the retailer' and includes it among the items of labour that must be counted in the calculation of value, although the functions performed by such labour are not explicitly taken into consideration.[16]

On the one hand then, Ricardo seems to consider irrelevant those costs that Marx would consider pure circulation costs;[17] on the other

---

[15] Ricardo, *On the Principles of Political Economy*, p. 264.

[16] Ibid., p. 25. In his *Essay on the Production of Wealth*, published in 1821, R. Torrens discusses the 'commercial sector' at length. He, like Ricardo, considers transport one of the activities of this sector. In listing the employees dependent on merchants, however, Torrens includes shop assistants and clerks, as well as sailors, coachmen, boatmen, and dockers.

[17] The importance Marx attributes to the analysis of circulation and the costs related to it, in contrast to Ricardo, must certainly be related to the idea of 'anarchy', central to Marx's portrayal of capitalism. The 'metamorphoses' of capital from its commodity to money form, i.e. the realization of the surplus-value extracted in production, constitutes a *permanent* problem for the capitalists, which entails average costs that cannot be reduced to a negligible minimum.

hand, on the one occasion on which he mentions them, he definitely includes them in value. Marx observes in this connection: 'The great economists, such as Smith, Ricardo, etc., are perplexed over mercantile capital being a special variety, since they consider the basic form of capital, capital as industrial capital, ... The rules concerning the formation of value, profit, etc., immediately deduced by them from their study of industrial capital, do not extend directly to merchants' capital. For this reason, they leave merchants' capital entirely aside and mention it only as a kind of industrial capital.'[18]

Ricardo's failure to classify costs the way Marx did is not difficult to explain. The distinction between the production of commodities and production in general, which underlies Marx's analysis of costs, was never as fundamental or explicit for Ricardo, although it is present (see for example his letter to Trower quoted in the introduction). Furthermore, the central objective of Ricardo's theory was the determination of the rate of profit. But once attention is focused on observable magnitudes, the distinction between production costs and pure circulation costs loses all significance. The quantities of labour, both direct and indirect, required for the circulation of commodities are then costs for the capitalists and therefore form part of the outlays on which profit must be measured; they therefore must be considered on the same footing as the labour required for production.[19]

3. Pure Costs of Circulation

Some further, secondary observations on commercial costs are still necessary. Marx argues repeatedly that commercial capital draws its profits and recovers its advances for pure circulation costs from

[18] *Capital* Volume 3, pp. 324-5.

[19] On the subject of Marx's distinction between productive and unproductive labour, see the following recently published studies: I. Gough, 'Productive and Unproductive Labour', in *New Left Review*, no. 76, 1972; J. Harrison, 'Productive and Unproductive Labour in Marx's Political Economy', in *Bulletin of the Conference of Socialist Economists*, 1973, pp. 70-81; A. Berthoud, *Travail productif et productivité du travail chez Marx*, Paris, 1974; C. Pelosi, *Marx sul lavoro produttivo e improduttivo*, Rome, 1974. See also the articles on this subject in numbers 10, 11, and 12 of the review *Critiques de l'économie politique*, 1973.

industrial surplus-value, which is thereby reduced. It follows that the general rate of profit is lower than it would be if pure circulation costs did not exist. On the other hand, commercial capital makes it possible to concentrate the operations required for the distribution of commodities; it thus represents a source of saving for total capital compared with a situation in which distribution is the direct responsibility of the industrial capitalists. In other words, we have a 'double reduction in profit for the industrial capitalist', first because of the profit of the commercial capitalist, second because of the repayment of his advances. 'But', Marx continues, 'owing to economizing and concentration which are bound up with division of labour, it shrinks less than it would if he himself had to advance this capital. The reduction in the rate of profit is less, because the capital thus advanced is less.'[20]

Let us now turn to the workers concerned with distribution. They are wage-earners just like production workers. For them, too, wages are determined by the cost of production of labour-power. But 'the application of this labour-power, its exertion, expenditure of energy, and wear and tear, is as in the case of every other wage-labourer by no means limited by its value'.[21] However, a commercial worker yields a return on the capital that employs him: 'He creates no direct surplus-value, but adds to the capitalist's income by helping him to reduce the cost of realizing surplus-value, inasmuch as he performs partly unpaid labour.'[22] To the commercial capitalist who employs them these workers *appear* to be productive. In fact, for 'the merchant they [costs of circulation] appear as a source of profit, proportional, given the general rate of profit, to their size. The outlay to be made for these circulation costs is, therefore, a productive investment *for mercantile capital*. And for this reason, the commercial labour which it buys is likewise immediately productive *for it*'.[23]

---

[20] *Capital* Volume 3, p. 297.

[21] Ibid., p. 300.

[22] Ibid., p. 300.

[23] Ibid., p. 301 (emphasis added). This passage is immediately preceded by the following assertion: 'To industrial capital the costs of circulation *appear as* unproductive expenses, *and so they are*' (emphasis added). In my view Marx does not properly justify this difference between the commercial and industrial view of circulation costs. In the passage cited above, the fact that workers employed by

In these passages two definitions of productive labour are brought together; the first is based on participation in the production process, while the second distinguishes between workers who produce surplus-value and those who do not. The logical priority of the first of these definitions over the second is evident. The productive character of the labour of the commercial wage-earner is only apparent. Although as a wage-earner he *appears* to be a source of profit (because of the uniformity of the rate of profit), he produces no surplus-value since he does not actually produce anything at all.[24] On the other hand, all the social labour expended in the production of the 'constant' portion of commercial capital can be included in the general category of 'unproductive cost', in which Marx includes the labour expended in the production of gold used as money.[25] I would argue that Marx held two concepts of 'unproductive cost': unproductive cost in relation to a given commodity – that is, the labour directly expended on its pure circulation; and unproductive cost in general, including both the labour used indirectly for pure circulation (materials used by the commercial capitalists) and the labour expended in the production of gold, which serves as money. Only costs unproductive in the first sense are excluded from the value of the total product.

One additional point should be made in this connection. As we have seen, pure circulation costs also include expenditure on materials. This expenditure, like the direct labour necessary, does not become part of the value of the commodities that require such

commercial capital appear productive is ascribed to the fact that the capitalist makes a profit at a uniform rate on advances for their wages. But the same appearance should pertain for the circulation costs regularly incurred by industrial capitalists. The general criterion that seems to consolidate Marx's views most consistently would appear to be this: all pure circulation costs considered normal, whether incurred by industrial or commercial capitalists, and upon which the rate of profit is calculated, appear as productive. On the problem of the plausibility of an identical rate of profit for commercial and industrial capital, which is Marx's hypothesis, see A. Roncaglia, Introduction to R. Torrens, *Saggio sulla produzione richezza*, Milan, 1972, p. xxiv.

[24] For a completely opposite interpretation of the above quotation, see Pelosi, p. 129. Pelosi seems to hold that Marx's definition of productive labour from the capitalist viewpoint is this: for a worker to be productive it is necessary and *sufficient* for him to be a wage-earner. Thus workers employed in circulation would also be productive, provided they earn a wage. But Marx is explicit on this point: they are and appear unproductive if employed by industrial capitalists; they remain unproductive if employed by commercial capitalists, although they do not seem so.

[25] *Capital* Volume 2, pp. 213-214.

expenditure for their circulation. The problem then arises, which Marx did not consider, of whether the labour expended in the production of the materials that are then employed for pure circulation is productive labour or not. It would appear that the reply should be affirmative: anyone who produces equipment used by a commercial capitalist for book-keeping produces 'product and value', even though he does not produce, whether directly or indirectly, the commodities that require the use of this equipment for their distribution.

4. Socially Necessary Labour and Market-Value (i)

One of Marx's observations on differential rent and the price of agricultural products contains an explicit reference to the principle of real cost and a clear distinction between the actual cost of commodities and what appears to be their cost as a result of competition. Before we proceed to the passage that interests us most directly, however, we must pause to consider the preliminary concept of 'market-value', which is of considerable intrinsic importance in the context of our argument.

In discussing the magnitude of value, Marx makes it clear that this must be calculated on the basis of 'the labour time which is necessary on an average, or in other words is socially necessary. Socially necessary labour-time is the labour-time required to produce any use-value under the conditions of production normal for a given society and with the average degree of skill and intensity of labour prevalent in that society'.[26] 'Necessary on an average' therefore means necessary under socially 'normal' conditions. We are therefore dealing with an average of magnitudes that are generally identical or very close to the average itself. This interpretation is confirmed by Marx's discussion of the transition from a given method of production to a more efficient one.[27] Relative surplus-value, Marx argues, arises from the reduction in value of the material components of variable capital, which in turn originates in changes in production techniques in the industries producing wage-

---

[26] *Capital* Volume 1, p. 129.
[27] See the discussion on relative surplus-value, *Capital* Volume 1, pp. 432-35.

goods, whether directly or indirectly. He describes such changes in some detail; it all begins with the introduction of a new production method by an individual capitalist in a given industry. The immediate result is this: 'The individual value of these articles is now below their social value; in other words, they have cost less labour-time than the great bulk of the same article produced under the average social conditions.' By virtue of this difference the innovating capitalist appropriates 'an extra surplus-value'. As this more efficient method is imitated by other industrial capitalists, however, the average price falls to the level of the individual value, which has now become social, in accordance with the new method; the extra surplus-value thereby disappears.[28]

At the end of this chapter we will return to Marx's description of this process. For the moment it is sufficient to note that both before and immediately after the introduction of the new method (when the amount produced under this method is still insignificant compared with total output), industry as a whole is characterized by a method of production and a corresponding labour-time through which 'most of the output' is obtained: the average labour-time is therefore common to the great majority of producers and is thus the norm.

Both the definition of socially necessary labour-time and the discussion of the transition from one method of production to another within a given industry seem to imply a view of the process of accumulation which, as presented in *Capital* Volume 1, may be roughly summarized as follows. The development of any given industry is divided into periods, each of which is characterized by the predominance of a particular method of production simultaneously adopted by the great majority of producers in that industry, which thereby becomes the 'socially normal' method of production; the socially necessary labour-time corresponds to this method. This time is also the average necessary labour-time, since the proportion of the total product of the industry obtained by methods other than the normal one is insignificant. The period of transition from one to a more efficient method is accorded only fleeting analysis. Marx speaks of a social value (socially necessary labour-time) corresponding to the old method and a social value corresponding to the new

---

[28] The term average price refers to the point around which market prices fluctuate. As we have already noted in the introduction, Marx often omits the intermediate term between value and actual average price, namely the price of production.

method, but not of a social value during the period of transition itself (when, for example, the quantities produced under the old and new method may be roughly equal).

The co-existence of varying production methods within a single industry is, however, accorded greater weight in Volume 3, particularly in chapter 10 and in the discussion of differential rent. The central concept here is that of market-value, which at first sight seems to be defined in the same manner as socially necessary labour. It is a question of the average of individual magnitudes relative to overall production of a given commodity. In Volume 3, however, the average (the market-value) is no longer the magnitude that corresponds to the individual figure for the the great majority of producers, as was the case in Volume 1. Instead we have an average of widely varying magnitudes of labour that account for the production of significant proportions of the total output of the industry in question. Marx divides the various capitals operating in any one industry into three portions: that operating under average conditions, that whose productivity is higher than average, and that whose productivity is less than average. Moreover, the sectors operating above and below average are not unimportant, nor do they necessarily offset each other.[29] The market-value is unambiguously defined as the weighted average of the individual values. Speaking of the case in which the sector with lower than average productivity is larger than the sector with higher than average productivity, Marx writes: 'Strictly speaking, the average price, or the market-value, of each individual commodity, or each aliquot part of the total mass, would now be determined by the total value of the mass as obtained by adding up the values of the commodities produced under different conditions, and in accordance with the aliquot part of this total value falling to the share of each individual commodity.' He then examines the opposite case, in which: 'The average value, computed by adding the sums of values at the two extremes and at the middle, stands here below the value of the middle, which it approaches, or vice versa, depending on the relative place occupied by the favourable extreme.'[30]

[29] One of the cases examined by Marx is this: 'Suppose, finally, that the mass of commodities produced under better than average conditions considerably exceeds that produced under worse conditions, and is large even compared with that produced under average conditions'. (*Capital* Volume 3, p. 183.)

[30] Ibid., pp. 184.

In Volume 1 the average price – the magnitude around which market prices vary – is determined by the magnitude of value, defined as socially necessary labour, which means the labour required under socially normal conditions of production. The same is true for market-value as defined in Volume 3: market prices vary around this magnitude.[31] Now, in the case of socially necessary labour as defined in Volume 1, conditions of production are considered roughly homogeneous in the given industry; therefore, no problem arises from the identification of average price and average necessary labour, the latter being identical with the labour required in most units of production. If, on the other hand, there is a significant stratification of levels of productivity within the given industry, the weighted average of values produced by individual units does not appear to play a dominant role in the determination of the average price. There are then two possibilities. First, the situation in the industry is temporary, and eventually most production will be effected through the method yielding the highest productivity. In that case there is no sense talking about a price around which the market price varies, for an average magnitude of this sort will emerge only when the industry has been restructured. Or, second, the stratification of the industry is stable, access to the more efficient methods being blocked, for example by the great amount of capital required for reconversion.[32] In the case of an 'oligopolistic industry' of this type, the determination of the average price is linked in a very complex way to the structure of the industry and the breadth of the market: here again, market-value does not appear to be an important magnitude.[33]

We shall shortly see that elsewhere, when he deals with the formation of prices in industries characterized by a stable stratification, Marx's argumentation is linked to the specific problem at hand – and the weighted average of individual values finds no place in that argument. But in chapter 10 of Volume 3,

[31] For the identification of average price and value in Volume 1 see note 24 of chapter 5, p. 269, which has already been mentioned. For the determination of average price from market-value in Volume 3, see chapter 10 pp. 185-94.

[32] The other important case of stable stratification is agricultural production on lands of varying fertility, which we will examine later.

[33] For the minimum amount of capital required, see the passages in Volume 1 on the concentration that accompanies accumulation (pp. 775-777).

where value is identified with average price, the logic of real cost is predominant. All the hours of labour expended – under the various conditions of productivity – in the production of the total quantity of the commodity are added together and divided by the number of items produced. The result is the average labour-time it costs society to produce one item. On the one hand there is the strict calculation of the cost of the commodities in labour, on the other the figure around which market prices vary, the average price. The logic that guides Marx his elaboration of the first magnitude takes priority over consideration of the forces that cause observable changes of prices when he comes to determine the second.

5. Variations in Market-Value: Agriculture and Mining

The concept of market-value is developed differently in Marx's discussion of the price of agricultural products. So far, market-value has been defined as the average necessary labour, and the average price is 'necessarily' identified with it. When discussing the value of agricultural production, Marx seems to proceed in the opposite direction. Here the point of departure is the average price as determined by methods of production and the effects of competition, and the market-value is defined so as to coincide with it. Before examining the core of Marx's theory of rent, it is important to note that the many pages devoted to this subject in *Capital* Volume 3 and *Theories of Surplus Value* Volume 2 are the most obviously tentative of all of Marx's posthumously published writings, both in the vagueness of their content and in the lack of precision of their terminology.

In most cases Marx argues as follows in discussing the price of agricultural products. The labour expended on the least fertile land is considered the market-value. The cost price (constant plus variable capital) on that land, plus the general rate of profit, is the price of production. The latter is always lower than the market-value, since the organic composition of capital in agriculture is lower than the average for society as a whole. Because of the monopoly over the land held by the landowning class, the value of the agricultural product is not transformed into the price of production. The difference between value and price of production constitutes the absolute rent, which goes to all landowners without distinction.[34]

Again in *Theories of Surplus Value* Volume 2, embodied labour for the least fertile land is most often considered the market-value. There are, however, a few cases in which a different magnitude emerges. Marx considers, for example, mines of differing levels of productivity. To begin with he imagines three mines which, with an identical advance of capital of £100, produce 60, 65, and 75 tons of coal respectively in a given period of time. A new mine is then discovered which, with the same advance of capital, produces 92½ tons. Marx discusses the various situations that may arise as a result of the discovery of the new mine. In the first case, the total quantity produced remains the same, 200 tons; the first mine is closed and the second produces below its maximum capacity — 32½ tons instead of 65. The market-value then sinks to the level of individual value in this second mine. Under a second hypothesis, on the other hand, Marx supposes that the amount of coal the market can absorb will vary according to its price. If the reduction in price required to sell 292½ tons is not such as to drive the price below the price of production in the least productive mine, 'the total capital can continue to work in this sphere of production at this new market-value'.[35]

We shall not discuss these aspects of Marx's theory as they concern the analysis of competition and demand. What is of interest to us here is that the investigation of market-value now takes a different tack, for it is no longer defined as a weighted average. In both cases — when value is defined at the margin of production and when it is a magnitude lying between the extremes — Marx is guided by the study of the forces of competition rather than by the logic that prevails in chapter 10 of *Capital* Volume 3. But this logic crops up again in a comment that interrupts the exposition of differential rent in *Capital* Volume 3. The total product, Marx writes, amounts to 10 quarters. These are sold at 600 shillings, because the price of each quarter is determined on the worst land. But the 'real price of

---

[34] For a critique of Marx's theory of rent, see L. Meldolesi, introd. to Bortkeiwicz, *La teoria economica di Marx*, Turin, 1971.

[35] *Theories of Surplus-Value* Volume 2, London, 1969, p. 292. A table covering all the cases examined by Marx for quantity produced and market-value is on p. 264. In the example cited here, Marx has market-value fall below individual value in the least productive mines but keeps it above the price of production. All the capitalists get the same rate of profit, but the owners of the least productive mines do not receive all the *absolute* rent (see Table C, p. 264).

production' is only 240 shillings, and this is the average of all the prices of production on the various lands. The market-value established on the basis of competition is therefore a 'false social value'.[36]

6. Socially Necessary Labour and Market-Value (ii)

Let us return to Marx's description (in the chapter of *Capital* Volume 1 devoted to relative surplus-value) of the transition from one to another, more efficient method of production in a given industry. As we have said, this process begins when an innovating capitalist introduces a technique that allows him to reduce his unit costs. The price begins to fall because costs can be reduced under this new method only if the scale of production is increased. Marx is not explicit on this point, but no other interpretation of the example he constructs seems possible.[37] To obtain a larger share of the market, the innovating capitalist sells his commodities 'above their individual but below their social value'.[38] However, as the new method becomes more widely used, 'the difference between the individual value of the cheapened commodity and its social value vanishes'.[39]

This line of argument requires comment. To explain the fall in value Marx appeals to the forces of competition. But this shifts the discussion to actual exchange-values and necessarily requires

[36] *Capital* Volume 3, pp. 660-1. In the entire chapter from which these pages are taken Marx speaks not of value but of price of production, since he is leaving aside absolute rent; in other words, he is temporarily assuming that the value of agricultural products undergoes the same transformation as other values (ibid., p. 640). But in contrasting real price of production to false social value, all that matters is the difference between the calculation on the margin and the calculation based on the average. In any event, immediately after comparing the two magnitudes, Marx speaks of the 240 shillings as representing a quantity of labour. On the very same page, the calculation based on the average is presented as the basis on which the agricultural product would be assessed if 'the capitalist form of society' were replaced by a 'conscious association'. See note 8 of the introduction.

[37] 'On the other hand, [for the innovating capitalist] the working day of 12 hours is now represented, for him, by twenty-four articles instead of twelve. Hence, in order to get rid of the product of one working day, the demand must be double what it was, i.e. the market must become twice as extensive.' (*Capital* Volume 1, p. 434.)

[38] Ibid.

[39] Ibid., p. 436.

consideration of the rate of profit. The operation of competition as Marx sees it can account for the downward trend of the price, but not its stabilization at a particular new average level. A result of this type can be obtained only if prices of production themselves are considered. Once a new technique has been introduced and generalized throughout a given industry, the new average price level will be determined – simultaneously with that of other commodities – by the movement of capital in search of the highest rate of profit and by the resulting tendency of the rate of profit to uniformity. The expansion of the scale of production – which Marx introduces as an assumption – is not at all necessary if the problem is conceived in this way. It is, however, essential in explaining the tendency of the price to fall – though not sufficient to determine its new level – if, like Marx, one takes account only of competition among capitalists in a given industry, disregarding possible shifts of capital from one industry to another.

In this chapter on relative surplus-value, Marx seems to carry his substitution of values for prices of production to illegitimate lengths, thereby confusing different levels of investigation. We must also remember that the line of argument we are discussing here is preceded by a warning that the analysis of competition will have to be postponed.[40]

One more observation is needed on Marx's identification of market-value with average price in chapter 10 of Volume 3. Here again 'value' stands for 'price of production', as is shown by the passage from chapter 10 quoted in the introduction, where Marx points out that what is true for market-value is equally true for market price of production. Marx merely alludes to this in passing, as though it were self-evident. According to him, market prices of production should be formed on the basis of market-values in accordance with the transformation process suggested in chapter 9 of Volume 3. The general rate of profit in each industry is said to be attained only by those capitals operating under average conditions, while the others obtain either extra or sub-normal profits.

The points made in section 4 of this chapter also hold for the identification of market prices of production and average prices. Marx's assertion that market prices of production constitute the

---

[40] Ibid., p. 433.

levels around which market prices vary might suggest that he considered the stratification of industries stable. This, however, contradicts the uniformity of the rate of profit, which is the basis of the formation of market prices of production. If there are obstacles in each industry that prevent the advent of homogeneity, then the movement of capital between industries, which is the precondition for the equalization of the rate of profit, must be reconsidered.[41]

[41] In his *Sraffa e la teoria dei prezzi*, Bari, 1975, A. Roncaglia has examined the question of the stratification of industries (pp. 36-39). He maintains that the system of prices of production can also be used to analyse a 'period of technological transition', and gives two examples: a dominant technology that has not yet absorbed its predecessor and the opposite case, in which 'an innovation has barely been introduced'. In the first case, the price of production is calculated on the basis of the new technology, in the second according to the old one. Roncaglia's examples are important, since for him prices of production are not mere definitions but axes around which the fluctuations Marx discusses occur. But in the first case this is true only if the amount of the product still produced under the old technology is very small; in the second case only if the capitalists using the new technology are still making only a small contribution to the total output of the industry. But during the entire intermediary period (the greater part of the 'technological transition'), when both technologies produce considerable amounts of the commodity in question, prices of production can be of no use, however they are calculated. In the portions of his work discussed here, Roncaglia uses Marx's concepts of socially necessary labour-time and market-value. But he seems not to grasp the difference between the two; indeed, of the various cases Marx examines in his discussion of market-value, Roncaglia cites only that in which commodities produced under average conditions for their respective spheres of production constitute the greater portion of total output.

II
The 'Law of Nature'

1. Labour as Positive Activity

In examining Marx's exposition of the magnitude of value in *Capital*, we have seen that he introduces into the analysis elements of a 'theory of production' that logically precedes the theory of commodity production and exchange. In particular, because of his exclusion of circulation costs and because of his theory of market-value, Marx develops the principle of real cost independent of the problem of actual exchange ratios. We shall now look at certain passages of the *Grundrisse* in which Marx examines the idea of labour as 'real price', as formulated by Adam Smith.

Marx quotes a passage from chapter 5 of *The Wealth of Nations* in which Smith identifies labour − described as the sacrifice of 'rest', 'freedom', and 'happiness' − with 'real price'[1] and argues that Smith's idea of labour as sacrifice gave rise to Senior's attempt to introduce the notion of the capitalists' abstinence: 'This is why Mr Senior, for example, was able to make capital into a source of production in the same sense as labour, a source *sui generis* of the production of *value*, because the capitalist too brings a *sacrifice*, the sacrifice of *abstinence*, in that he grows wealthy instead of eating up his product directly.'[2]

---

[1] 'Equal quantities of labour, at all times and places, may be said to be of equal value to the labourer. In his ordinary state of health, strength and spirits; in the ordinary degree of his skill and dexterity, he must always lay down the same portion of his ease, his liberty and his happiness.' *An Inquiry into the Nature and Causes of the Wealth of Nations*, New York, 1937, p. 33. Marx also quotes the continuation of this passage, in which Smith contrasts 'real price' and 'nominal price'.

[2] *Grundrisse*, Penguin Books in association with New Left Review, Harmondsworth, 1973, p. 612.

Let us try to determine the logical structure of Marx's argument in these passages of the *Grundrisse*. The reason it becomes possible from Smith's point of view to include sacrifice among the sources of value is that he considered sacrifice the quality that makes labour the real cost of all things. But: 'Something that is merely negative [i.e. sacrifice] creates nothing.'[3] And: 'The *natural price* of things is not the sacrifice made for them.'[4] What makes labour the natural price of things is that it is '*a positive, creative activity*'.[5] Marx does not criticize the identification of labour and 'real price'.[6] Rather, he argues that Smith's error was to have considered labour a sacrifice.[7] It is important to note that Marx discusses what may or may not create value on the terrain of production in general, for the two qualities of labour contrasted here are not restricted to labour that produces commodities. Sacrifice does not create value, because it does not create anything in general: 'The negation of tranquillity, as mere negation, ascetic sacrifice, creates nothing. *Someone may castigate and flagellate himself all day long like the monks etc., and this quantity of sacrifice he contributes will remain totally worthless.*'[8] On the other hand, once labour is considered a positive activity, its products are nothing but crystalized labour: 'Use value is not concerned with human activity as the source of the product, with its having been posited by human activity, but with its being for mankind. In so far as the product has a measure for itself, it is its natural measure as natural object, mass, weight, ... But as effect, or as static presence of the force which created it, it is measured only by the measure of this force itself. The measure of labour is time. Only because products ARE labour can they be measured by the measure of labour, by labour time, the amount of labour consumed in them.'[9]

[3] Ibid., p. 612.

[4] Ibid., p. 613.

[5] Ibid., p. 614.

[6] Similarly, when Marx comments in *Theories of Surplus Value* on Smith's theory of real price, he criticizes *only* Smith's confusion between the quantity of objectified labour a commodity can buy and the quantity of living labour its possessor can utilize. (*Theories of Surplus-Value*, London, 1969, Volume 1, pp. 75-77.)

[7] On the other hand, Smith 'is right, of course, that, in its historic forms as slave-labour, serf-labour, and wage-labour, labour always appears as repulsive, always as *external forced labour*'; and not-labour, by contrast, as "freedom, and happiness"'. (*Grundrisse*, p. 611.) For the same point, see also *Capital* Volume 1, note 16, pp. 137-8.

[8] *Grundrisse*, p. 613.

[9] Ibid., p. 613.

As a use-value, an object is something to be used by man, capable of satisfying certain needs and thus endowed with certain natural properties. The natural process from which it emerges must therefore be tailored to the goal of obtaining just those qualities; and labour, which is part of that process, must assume the particular form required. But as a product – not something *for man*, but something made *by man* – an object is merely a manifestation of that positive, creative activity called labour; and its measure in labour expresses *how much* of that activity has been required to overcome the obstacles to its production: 'Certainly, labour obtains its measure from the outside, through the aim to be attained and the obstacles to be overcome in attaining it.'[10]

On the one hand, then, the measure of an object in labour terms is presented as a measure of the difficulties encountered in its production. On the other hand, such a measure presupposes some standard by which the various human labours applied to the same goal can be quantitatively compared – namely the average time required to carry out the particular operations. This sort of measurement reaches its apex in the production of commodities, since here, for the first time, the human labour supplied by different individuals is systematically related to an average social labour. 'We will examine elsewhere', Marx writes in the *Grundrisse*, 'to what extent this *measurement* is linked with exchange, not with organized social labour.'[11]

Underlying the concept of value, then, is the idea of the product as crystalized human labour. This is, so to speak, the aspect Marx considers obvious, already well known to classical political economy; what must still be clarified — and this, Marx holds, is the

---

[10] Ibid., p. 611.
[11] Ibid., p. 613. In other words, prior to capitalism, the measurement of products in labour and the equalization of varying individual labour times, which is its prerequisite, exist only *potentially*. Only under capitalism are they fully actualized: 'Bourgeois society is the most developed and the most complex historic organization of production. The categories which express its relations, the comprehension of its structure, thereby also allows insights into the structure and the relations of production of all the vanished social formations out of whose ruins and elements it built itself up, whose partly still unconquered remnants are carried along within it, whose mere nuances have developed explicit significance within it, etc. Human anatomy contains a key to the anatomy of the ape.' (Ibid., p. 105; from the 1857 'introduction' to *A Contribution to the Critique of Political Economy*.)

limitation of classical political economy – is the socio-historic context within which the labour embodied in products becomes value: 'Political economy has indeed analysed value and its magnitude, however incompletely, and has uncovered the content concealed within these forms. But it has never once asked the question why this content has assumed that particular form, that is to say, why labour is expressed in value, and why the measurement of labour by its duration is expressed in the magnitude of the value of the product.'[12]

The entire question is presented quite clearly in the *Critique of the Gotha Programme*. In the 'co-operative society', the 'individual producer receives back from society – after the deductions have been made – exactly what he gives to it'. And further on: 'But one man is superior to another physically or mentally and so supplies more labour in the same time, or can labour for a longer time; . . . This *equal* right is an unequal right for unequal labour.' Thus, 'in the first phase of communist society as it is when it has just emerged after prolonged birth pangs from capitalist society', the labour of different individuals is reduced to average social labour. Moreover, it is this reduction that determines the share of each individual in that portion of total social product earmarked for consumption. But, 'in contrast to capitalist society, individual labour no longer exists in an indirect fashion but directly as a component part of the total labour'.[13]

In other words, in the early stages of 'co-operative society' the products of social activity are still measured in terms of labour. Here, however, the reduction to equal labour of the particular labour of different individuals comes about as a conscious collective decision; in capitalist society, on the other hand, the same equalization occurs as the result of a process that unfolds behind the backs of the producers and therefore appears to them as a natural necessity.

The same theme is developed in the famous section of *Capital* devoted to 'commodity fetishism'. Here too Marx contrasts measurement in labour-time as it occurs in capitalist society with the planned distribution of social labour among various activities.

---

[12] *Capital* Volume 1, pp. 173-74.
[13] *Critique of the Gotha Programme*, in Marx-Engels, *Selected Works*, Moscow, 1962, Volume II, pp. 23-24.

Even an isolated individual like Robinson Crusoe on his island, Marx writes, knows that his various productive functions are 'only different modes of human labour. Necessity itself compels him to divide his time with precision between his different functions. Whether one function occupies a greater space in his total activity than another depends on the magnitude of the difficulties to be overcome in attaining the useful effect aimed at.... His stock-book contains a catalogue of the useful objects he possesses, of the various operations necessary for their production, and finally of the labour-time that specific quantities of these products have on average cost him.' Moreover, the relations between Robinson and the objects of his self-created wealth 'contain all the essential determinants of value'.[14]

It is therefore evident that Marx makes a distinction between labour as an objective social measure of the difficulties that impede the attainment of a given end (which is why it is necessary to refer to labour of average efficiency), and the way in which that measure is actually effected in accordance with the relations of production. The measure itself, be it noted, is in no way capitalist *per se*, although it attains its full development only with the generalization of commodity production. In other words, to fully understand labour as the substance of value three steps are required. First, labour must be seen as the manifestation of a generic human capacity to bend natural processes to human will, abstracting from the particular use to which this capacity is put. Second, all the various individual labours must be reduced to a social average through another abstraction (different from and subordinate to the first), this time from the varying levels of productivity consequent to the differing abilities of the individual workers or the different available tools. Third, this process of equalization must be seen as the result of a process alien to the conscious decisions of the producers themselves and imposed on them as an external necessity. The abstraction from the useful characteristics of different types of labour and from the variations among the individuals who perform them is required for any measure of the difficulties encountered in production. In capitalist society, however, this abstraction is not effected through the conscious regulation of social production; it

[14] *Capital* Volume 1, pp. 169-170.

therefore 'adheres to' the products of labour as their value. In the consciousness of the producers, it thereby appears as a natural quality of these products.[15]

To avoid misunderstanding, it is perhaps necessary to emphasize that there is a difference between labour as 'a measure of obstacles' and labour as 'the source of all wealth', for Marx opposed the latter characterization categorically.[16] In so far as it is considered as concrete, labour is only part of a process of interaction with nature and requires natural forces. The *social cost* of products, however, is determined solely by the labour expended to obtain them.

The explicit references in Marx's discussion of circulation costs, rent, and Smith's conception of labour as sacrifice have thus led us to recognize the centrality of the logic of production *per se* in Marx's approach. The principle of real cost belongs to his theory of production and has no counterpart in a general theory of distribution. This principle holds sway throughout the production of commodities, where it also dominates, although not directly, as a law of distribution. Even in the 'co-operative society' envisaged in the *Critique of the Gotha Programme* distribution is governed by relative contribution of labour. But here it is not a law but a conscious social decision. In the section on commodity fetishism in *Capital* Volume 1 Marx speaks of an imaginary 'association of free men' and assumes that the share of the means of subsistence received by each producer is determined by his labour-time – but 'only for the sake of a parallel with the production of commodities'.[17]

[15] In order not to overburden the discussion, we are deliberately ignoring the problem of the reduction to 'simple labour' of more complex labour that takes longer to learn. Marx viewed skilled labour as '*intensified*, or rather *multiplied* simple labour'. Since the reduction occurs behind the backs of the producers, it appears to them to have been 'handed down by tradition'. Marx does not explain the quantitative aspect of this reduction to simple labour with any precision, but it seems to be based on training costs. For example: 'All labour of a higher, or more complicated character than average labour is expenditure of labour-power of a more costly kind, labour-power whose production has cost more time and labour than unskilled or simple labour-power, and which therefore has a higher value.' (*Capital* Volume 1, p. 305.) The different *values* of differently qualified labour-power, Marx immediately remarks in a footnote, are not necessarily reflected by the market. The inclusion of training costs in assessing the value of complex labour enables the process of training skilled labour-power to be seen as a moment in the indirect production of the use-values in whose production this labour-power participates directly.

[16] See, for example, *Critique of the Gotha Programme*, pp. 18-19.

[17] *Capital* Volume 1, pp. 171-172.

2. Abstract Labour

While on the subject of Marx's concept of abstract labour, it is opportune to discuss the thesis advanced by Lucio Colletti in his essay 'Bernstein and the Marxism of the Second International'.[18] We agree with one aspect of his interpretation: the abstract labour that Marx holds to be the substance of value is not the product of a mental generalization based on the various types of particular labour; rather, what is needed is a positive definition that embodies the historical and social features that make labour productive of value. Colletti argues that the whole significance of abstract labour, the labour that produces value, lies in its equalization of different types of human labour, which is then expressed as value.[19]

It is my view that Colletti does not distinguish sharply enough between two aspects of the question. Measurement in labour-time of the obstacles to be overcome in production necessarily requires reference to labour of average efficiency, to some sort of equalization. This applies to measurement in labour as such, regardless of the particular historical character of social relations. In capitalist society, this equalization occurs through labour's becoming value, with the consequent separation of labour from the subject who performs it. The abstraction, however, lies not in the equalization as such but only in the way it occurs, as Marx makes clear in the passage from the *Critique of the Gotha Programme* quoted above.

In other words, the various particular labours are so many manifestations of the creative capacity that is human labour-power. This labour-power, far from being a mental generalization, represents the generic character of the natural being man, his ability to act in accordance with natural laws, and can be positively defined in terms of its component functions, 'brains, muscles, nerves, hands, etc.',[20] always viewed historically, of course. In

---

[18] In Lucio Colletti, *From Rousseau to Lenin – Studies in Ideology and Society*, NLB, London, 1972.

[19] 'Unlike those interpreters who think it is obvious and non-problematical that in commodity production each individual labour-power is considered as a "human labour power identical to all others" or as "average social labour power", and hence have never asked themselves what this equalization of labour signifies – unlike them, I believe that this is precisely where the significance of "abstract labour" and the entire theory of value is to be found.' (Ibid., p. 84.)

[20] 'Tailoring and weaving, although they are qualitatively different productive activities, are both a productive expenditure of human brains, muscles, nerves, hands, etc., and in this sense both human labour. They are merely two different forms of the expenditure of human labour-power'. (*Capital* Volume 1, p. 134.)

considering objects as products, measurement in labour (as a measure of difficulty) is characteristic of associated human action, regardless of the historical form assumed by the relations of production: '*Labour-time*, even if exchange-value is eliminated, *always remains* the creative substance of wealth and the measure of the *cost* of its production.'[21] This raises the problem of the reduction of various types of human labour. When the products of labour are commodities, which means that the different types of labour are performed privately, measurement in labour and reduction to measurable units come about through exchange.

It is important to emphasize that the general expenditure of labour-power we are talking about here as a measure of the difficulties encountered in production *is not* a mental abstraction from various particular activities, for such an abstraction would not give us a *quantity*. On the contrary, when labour is thought of as a measure of obstacles, then the various particular activities become forms of a positive and measurable entity: the universal human capacity for labour.

Colletti explains the meaning of abstract labour by comparing a primitive community to a society of commodity production, using the example with which Marx illustrated the concept of socially necessary labour. After the introduction of the steam-powered loom, one hour of labour on the hand loom equals only half an hour of labour of average efficiency. Now, this sort of equalization is not necessarily exclusive to commodity production. To begin with, we must distinguish between genuine individual differences among workers and differences due to the variety of the tools employed (as in the case to which Colletti refers). Let us now, following Marx in the *Critique of the Gotha Programme*, shift to a 'co-operative society' in which workers receive varying shares of

---

[21] *Theories of Surplus-Value* Volume 3, London, 1969, p. 257. This assertion is taken from Marx's summary of the ideas of the anonymous author of the pamphlet *The Source and Remedy of the National Difficulties*, one of the works examined in the chapter entitled 'Opposition to the Economists (based on the Ricardian Theory)'. Marx continues thus: 'But free time, *disposable time*, is wealth itself, partly for the enjoyment of the product, partly for free activity which – unlike labour – is not dominated by the pressure of an extraneous purpose which must be fulfilled, and the fulfilment of which is regarded as a natural necessity or a social duty, according to one's inclination.' Marx's total commitment to this position is clear from the context; moreover, the same theme is developed in the passages of the *Grundrisse* discussed above.

total social product depending on their varying contributions of labour. Here Marx is referring to the average times set for the performance of given tasks and to different individual labour-times. The notion of average necessary labour-time arises spontaneously from the need to plan social production on an industrially developed base, which naturally entails an equalization independent of the individual capacity of each worker. But this sort of equalization entails no *separation*.

If, however, the labour of a worker in this 'co-operative society' is less efficient than average, it is reduced, when it comes to *measuring costs*, to a fraction of the time actually spent on the job. In Marx's 'model', this would lead to lower payment. But this does not mean that the labour is 'estranged' from the worker who performs it. Indeed, both the equalization and the difference in payment are based on a conscious social decision known to the worker, for he has helped to make it.

Moreover, the labour of each individual worker is immediately social in that it is an element of the plan. As an expenditure of generic activity, such labour must be reduced to an average. But this average is only the result of an explicit comparison of various individual capacities effected by the producers themselves; it does not occur implicitly, as in commodity production, where it is imposed on them through a mechanism alien to them.[22]

Let us now consider the other case, in which the difference in productivity is caused by the introduction of new machines. It is clear that even in a 'co-operative society', society will place less value on labour performed on old machines, and this could well take the form of a reduction in the price of products when more efficient machinery is introduced. But here again, what is lamentable is not so much the equalization as the fact that under commodity production it appears to those working on the now out-dated machinery as a gradual decline in the value of 'their' commodity and therefore as a compulsion to yield to the effects of decisions over which they have no control, under pain of outright exclusion from the market. In the 'co-operative society', on the other hand, the equalization appears to the workers as the result of their own decisions on production

---

[22] Actually, the relationship of the producers to their labour remains that of subject and attribute, although in social relations there is an equalization, with individual particularities disregarded.

methods.[23] In this second case, the 'rationality' of the equalization is particularly apparent and so, therefore, is the need to distinguish carefully between the fact of its occurrence and the manner in which it occurs.[24] We shall shortly return to Colletti's study to discuss another aspect of it.

3. The Fixity of 'Natural Law'

We began with the identification of value and labour in the opening pages of *Capital* and saw straightaway that value does not determine actual exchange ratios directly. Indeed, in Volumes 2 and 3 value becomes real cost and, as such, is counterposed to the magnitudes actually reflected in exchange. There is an important passage in which Marx strikingly combines the 'natural' basis of value and its link to these observable magnitudes. In his 11 July 1868 letter to Kugelmann, Marx states:

'All that palaver about the necessity of proving the concept of value comes from complete ignorance both of the subject dealt with and of scientific method. Every child knows that a nation which ceased to work, I will not say for a year, but even for a few weeks, would perish. Every child knows, too, that the masses of products corresponding to the different needs require different and quantitatively determined masses of the total labour of society. That this *necessity* of the *distribution* of social labour in definite proportions cannot possibly be done away with by a *particular form* of social production but can only change the *form* in which it *appears* is self-evident. No natural laws can be done away with. What can change, in historically different circumstances, is only the *form* in which these laws operate. And the *form* in which this

[23] In the 'co-operative society', of course, the different valuation of the labour performed with different tools does not affect the distribution of the social product as under commodity production.

[24] It is fitting to note here that it is from the work of Colletti that I, like many others, learnt exactly what Marx meant by abstract labour. The points made above result from Colletti's failure to distinguish explicitly between the equalization implicit in any measure in labour and the equalization in value. In this regard see *From Rousseau to Lenin*, pp. 91-92, in which Colletti quite rightly protests against the confusion between the 'law of labour-time' under socialism and the law of value under capitalism; but he does not clarify the problem of equalization implicit in this distinction.

proportional distribution of labour operates in a state of society where the interconnection of social labour is manifested in the *private exchange* of the individual products of labour, is precisely the *exchange-value* of these products. Science consists precisely in demonstrating *how* the law of value operates.'

This passage is immediately followed by clarification of what is meant by 'the *form* in which these laws operate'. Here we again have a twofold mediation linking quantities of labour to directly observable exchange-values. First, on the difference between values and production prices: 'So that if one wanted at the very beginning to "explain" all the phenomena which apparently contradict that law, one would have to present the science *before* the science. It is precisely Ricardo's mistake that in his first chapter on value he takes as given all possible categories which have still to be developed for us, in order to prove their conformity with the law of value.' Second, on the difference between average and market price: 'The vulgar economist has not the faintest idea that the actual everyday exchange relations *cannot be directly identical* with the magnitudes of value. The point of bourgeois society consists precisely in this, that *a priori* there is no conscious, social regulation of production. The rational and naturally necessary asserts itself only as a blindly working average.'[25]

Let us analyse this distinction between a 'natural law' and the 'form in which it operates' under various historical forms of production. Then we can connect this passage to our earlier discussion.

If we leave aside the social context in which commodities are produced and examine only the material aspect of the organic inter-relationship between men and nature, everything may be reduced to the distribution of labour among the various branches of production. More precisely, given available production methods, the composition of the use-values produced corresponds to the distribution of labour among the various sectors − this is the natural law Marx is talking about. (Both the distinction between circulation and production costs and the conception of the market-value of agricultural output as 'false social value' belong to this level of investigation.)

---

[25] *Marx-Engels Selected Works*, Moscow, 1962, Volume II, pp. 461-462.

At first sight, this abstraction, which disregards the commodity character of the products, seems a component of the reconstruction *in thought* of commodity production, since the material analysis of production is intertwined with that of the particular social relationships within which production occurs. On the other hand, again at a first sight, Marx seems to be propounding a proposition of this sort: the necessary consistency among the various branches of production will be asserted either *a priori*, through planning, or *a posteriori* (as in commodity production), through the signals that producers receive from prices.

But Marx's argumentation is actually far more 'weighty'. The material basis on which the production of commodities takes place plays a *causal* role in the determination of exchange relationships. A natural law 'operates' through the 'forms' characteristic of production. When objects become commodities, the social process escapes the control of the producer. As a result, things – the products – appear to the producers as imbued with a law of motion of their own – and so they are. But the more general law of the distribution of labour among the various branches of production must inevitably find expression in this law. It is thus labour, performed by mutually independent producers and measured as socially necessary labour, that dominates the movement of commodities, becoming their *substance* as values.[26] The fact that labour is the substance of *value*, that it functions as an entity imbued with a life of its own, results from the specific mode of production. But that value can be nothing but labour is, for Marx, another matter. In their mutual relations, whatever their form, men merely distribute the labour required to produce various articles. When the form of this relation is commodity exchange, men exchange labour,

---

[26] According to this view, labour is the 'substance' of objects to the extent that they are products: 'only because products *are* labour can they be measured by the quantity of labour'. Inasmuch as this measurement appears as purely natural and not as a conscious norm of the relationship between men and nature – since it results from a process independent of the conscious decisions of the producers – labour is the 'substance' of value. On this point see Colletti, 'Bernstein and the Marxism of the Second International', and Colletti, *Marxism and Hegel*, NLB, London, 1969, where it is shown that the same idea of 'real hypostatization' lies at the root of both the theory of commodity fetishism and the *Contribution to the Critique of Hegel's Philosophy of Right*. When we speak of the intuition that inspired Marx in the transformation of values into prices, it is to the first of these two notions of 'substance' that we are referring.

more or less indirectly, but they exchange labour nonetheless. In our discussion of *Capital* Volume 3 and the transformation of values into prices of production, we shall see that Marx's entire investigation of profit is dominated by the idea of the conservation-redistribution of aggregate magnitudes determined in the sphere of production. This is how the 'natural law' operates under commodity production, not immediately – through an identity of actual exchange-values and ratios of quantities of embodied labour – but in the 'last instance'.

Value simply translates into the language of commodities the human, active side of the material process through which these commodities have emerged from nature. The magnitude of value expresses their *real social cost*. Value is the form assumed by real social cost under commodity production. Capitalist competition, which is an element of the form in which production occurs, can only operate on the basis of magnitudes of value and surplus-value: the 'law' is asserted through the permanence of these quantities.

Let us recapitulate. Marx grounds the law of value in the need of commodity production to conform to a system of natural law. We have seen that he states this explicitly and have confirmed that it is consistent with aspects of his treatment of value in regard to circulation costs and the value of agricultural production. We have thus concluded that for Marx, labour is value *only* when it produces commodities and is therefore abstract labour; but it is value in given historical conditions *because* it is the real social cost of objects as products. The identification of labour – i.e., real cost – with value is closely connected to the assumption that the exchange ratios of commodities *can be reduced*, even if only indirectly, to quantities of labour. When Marx comes to consider prices of production, this assumption is reflected in the idea that the aggregate quantities of value and surplus-value are conserved. This point will be examined more fully in the following chapter.

In his letter to Kugelmann defining the scientific approach, Marx argues that on the basis of what all modes of production have in common, laws can be discovered that govern the exchange of commodities. Indeed, the 1857 introduction to *A Contribution to the Critique of Political Economy* calls attention to 'production in general'; described as 'an abstraction, but a rational abstraction in so far as it really brings out and fixes the common element and thus saves us repetition'. And: 'the elements which are not general and common, must be separated out from the determinations valid for production as such, so that in their unity – which arises already from the identity of the subject, humanity, and of the object, nature – their essential difference is not forgotten.'[27]

The significance of these remarks becomes considerably clearer in the letter to Kugelmann. There it is evident that Marx regards the foundation of value as among the set of 'determinations valid for production as such'. It is to this *causal* relationship between these determinations and the magnitude of value that we are referring when we speak of the 'naturalism' implicit in Marx's theory of value.[28]

4. 'The Law of Nature' and the Marxist Tradition

The line of argumentation under discussion here crops up frequently in Marxist tradition. It is opportune, then, to consider several particularly striking examples.

Rudolf Hilferding's reply to Böhm-Bawerk's study *Karl Marx and the Close of his System*[29] contains clear traces of it. Böhm-Bawerk started from the proposition that *Capital* Volume 3 introduced a contradiction in the theory of exchange-value as presented in Volume 1. Although he considered this alone sufficient to invalidate Marx's entire theoretical structure, he went on to investigate the 'deduction' of the opening pages of *Capital* in an attempt to demonstrate that the logic of the deduction was intrinsically fallacious. To disregard the specific forms in which use-value appears, he argued, is not the same as to disregard use-value in general, which is a characteristic of all commodities. Marx's method of reasoning, then, does not necessarily lead to the identification of the human labour that produced them as the quality common to all commodities. If Marx reaches this conclusion, it is only because of

---

[27] *Grundrisse*, p. 85.

[28] It should be noted that in my view this naturalism applies only to the determination of the *magnitude* of value. Marx's analysis of the form labour assumes under commodity production is *superimposed* on this determination.

[29] 'Böhm-Bawerk's Criticism of Marx', in Böhm-Bawerk, *Karl Marx and the Close of his System*, edited by Paul Sweezy, London, 1975.

his prior intention and not because he has correctly applied his own method.

To some extent it was easy to defend Marx against this charge. The fact is that Böhm-Bawerk was wide of the mark to claim that Volumes 1 and 3 were contradictory. It was easy to respond, as Hilferding did, by re-examining the transformation of values into production prices according to Marx's method. But neither Böhm-Bawerk nor Hilferding realized that this transformation itself posed serious difficulties. Hilferding in turn, however, did not simply deny that there was a contradiction between Volume 1 and Volume 3. He also advanced a positive exposition of the foundation of the law of value. The 'fundamental economic idea', namely the identity of value and labour, he maintained, is 'identical with the fundamental idea of the materialist conception of history'. The law of value applies to the 'epoch wherein labour and the power which controls labour have not been consciously elevated to the rank of a regulative principle of social metabolism and social predominance, but wherein this principle unconsciously and automatically establishes itself as a material quality of things'. Further: '*Society has, as it were, assigned to each of its members the quota of labour necessary to society; has specified to each individual how much labour he must expend.* And these individuals have forgotten what their quota was, and rediscover it only in the process of social life.'[30] Thus the 'principle' valid for any historical mode of production 'establishes itself' under commodity production.

Let us now consider another example. The chapter 'The Quantitative-Value Problem' in Paul Sweezy's book *The Theory of Capitalist Development* opens with the passage from Marx's letter to Kugelmann quoted above. Sweezy maintains that this constitutes the foundation of value as a magnitude; this magnitude, however, is merely a 'first approximation' of exchange ratios: 'Deviations which occur in practice can be dealt with in subsequent approximations to reality.'[31] Sweezy, whose book was first published in 1942, was thoroughly familiar with the Marxist tradition on this subject, but also with Bortkiewicz's studies of values and prices, which lie

---

[30] Ibid., pp. 133-34.
[31] *The Theory of Capitalist Development*, London, 1962, p. 42.

outside this tradition.[32] It is probable that this is the source of his presentation of value as a first approximation of exchange ratios, which was not at all necessary for someone like Hilferding, who held that the issue was merely the redistribution of surplus-value.

Let us attempt to clarify this question. As early as 1937, Maurice Dobb considered value a first approximation of actual exchange ratios. He then made this analogy: 'The theory of gravitation is not rendered absurd and useless merely because it requires substantial modification to explain why airships and aeroplanes can rise in the air.'[33] But the analogy is wholly inappropriate. The theory of gravitation requires no modification to account for the fact that some objects fly. On the contrary, it retains full validity, though gravity is not the only factor governing the motion of such objects. Indeed, the validity of the law of gravity is *confirmed* by the phenomena of aerodynamics, which are determined by a combination of gravity and other factors. According to Marx, this is precisely the relationship between the law of value and actual exchange ratios: the law is fully valid (which would not be true of a first approximation), since production prices can be derived through the interaction of the production of value and surplus-value and the redistribution of the latter as profit.[34] There is, then, no basis in Marx's work for the notion that value is a first approximation. Rather, this idea is a sign of weakness, a result of the growing awareness that his approach to value cannot be upheld in the terms in which it is formulated. We shall return to this whole question in chapter 4.

Finally, let us return to the study by Lucio Colletti that we looked at earlier. Colletti begins with the problem of Marx's method of exclusion raised by Böhm-Bawerk and notes that this criticism cannot be answered if abstract labour is considered a mental generalization by the investigator. He then sets out to uncover the *reality* of the

---

[32] See Bortkiewicz, 'On the Correction of Marx's Fundamental Theoretical Construction in the Third Volume of *Capital*', in *Karl Marx and the Close of his System*, and 'Wertrechnung und Preisrechnung in marxschen System', in *Archiv für Sozialwissenschaft und Sozialpolitik, 1906-1907*.

[33] Maurice Dobb, *Political Economy and Capitalism*, London, 1940 (second edition), p.17.

[34] The idea that the law of value undergoes modification belongs more to Ricardo, who also speaks of ratios of quantities of embodied labour as approximations to actual exchange-values. This was one of the reasons for Marx's criticism of him.

abstraction of labour in Marx's theory of commodity production. This, however, in no way constitutes an answer to Böhm-Bawerk, for his contention is that the identification of value with labour is invalid, an objection that cannot be refuted by clarifying the character of the labour Marx identifies with value. The labour of those employed in the distribution of commodities is no less abstract than that of workers who produce in the material sense. And yet Marx holds that their labour does not produce value, since it is not 'intrinsically productive'. The abstract character of labour corresponds to the commodity form of the product. But why it is precisely labour that constitutes the value of commodities is something else again, and concerns, Marx holds, production as such. Indeed, as we have already seen, 'political economy has analysed, however incompletely, value and its magnitude', although 'it has never once asked why labour is represented by the value of its product and labour-time by the magnitude of that value'. In other words, according to Marx, the discovery that labour underlies value was made before abstract labour was understood.

Colletti's study, while inspired by the need to correct the errors made by Marxists in their attempts to answer criticisms of the Böhm-Bawerk type, is therefore limited to the problem of what Marx means by abstract labour, thereby giving the impression that this provides the solution to all the problems related to value and labour. Indeed, discussion of the concept of abstract labour is far the most dominant element of Colletti's essay. The concomitant problem of why labour is value is relegated to two opening pages (pp. 77-78) in which Colletti more or less repeats the argument of Marx's letter to Kugelmann. But Colletti neither develops nor interprets Marx's argument. What is the significance of this argument for Marx? Nor does he subject it to criticism. Can the identity of value and labour legitimately be deduced from it?

The 'naturalism' implicit in Marx's reference to production in general has been well highlighted by Cesare Luporini in his *Dialettica e Materialismo*.[35] He recalls this same passage of the letter to Kugelmann and, inveighing against the trend initiated by Colletti, insists on the 'highly concrete physical' character of labour as the expenditure 'of physical and mental energy'.[36] Although I

[35] Rome, 1974.
[36] Ibid., pp. xiii-xv.

agree with Luporini's interpretation, his views on value are quite distant from the concrete scientific elaboration of historical materialism in *Capital*. Luporini discusses Marx's 'naturalism' without reference either to the positive propositions about exchange-values to which it is extended, or, consequently, to the difficulties it encounters whenever those propositions prove untenable.

III

Real Cost and Exchange-Value

The analysis of Marx's theory of prices of production presented in this chapter will emphasize that Marx considered this theory an extension and confirmation of the labour theory of value. As we shall see, Marx was explicit that this is his line of investigation, and he assumed that it could be realized. The labour embodied in commodities is thought of as a 'substance' (or 'energy' or 'fluid') with which they are imbued during production. It is from this image that the key idea that dominates Marx's method of determining prices is derived: the conservation of given quantities of this substance. The analysis that follows here is devoted to examining the presence and articulation of this 'measurable permanent substance' in *Capital* Volume 3.

As we shall see shortly, the discussion of the problem of profit throughout the first twelve chapters of *Capital* Volume 3 is closely connected to the critique of the idea that capital is the source of profit. In the next chapter this critical objective will be separated from the particular form in which it is pursued in *Capital*; this will enable us to draw some conclusions about the reconstruction of Marx's thought and the current direction of research on *Capital*.

1. Marx and the Origin of Profit

In chapter 9 of *Capital* Volume 3, having determined prices of production on the basis of a redistribution of total surplus-value, Marx synthesizes his argument up to this point as follows: 'The actual difference of magnitude between profit and surplus-value — not merely between the rate of profit and the rate of surplus-value – in the various spheres of production now completely conceals the true nature and origin of profit. . . . The transformation of values into prices of production serves to obscure the basis for determining value itself.' But this concealment occurs regardless of the uniformity of the rate of profit: 'since the mere transformation of surplus-value into profit distinguishes the portion of the value of a commodity forming the profit from the portion forming its cost-price, it is natural that the conception of value should elude the capitalist at this juncture, for he does not see the total labour put into the commodity, but only that portion of the total labour for which he has paid in the shape of means of production, be they living or not, so that his profit appears to him as something outside the immanent value of the commodity.' Moreover: 'This idea is fully confirmed, fortified and ossified', because of the uniformity of the rate of profit, which results in a quantitative difference between profit and surplus-value in the various spheres of production.[1]

The very first chapter of *Capital* Volume 3 opens with the assertion that the apparent derivation of profit from total capital results not only from the uniformity of the rate of profit, but also from the 'grouping of the various value portions of a commodity which only replace the value of the capital expended in its production under the head of cost price'.[2] Here profit is still quantitatively equal to surplus-value, but there is a change in its form: it is now surplus-value as it appears to those engaged in production. Value itself also undergoes a change in form: it is no longer $c + v + s$, but $k + p$, where $k = c + v$ and $p = s$. This means that the various elements of capital are unified and are, without distinction, advances of capital. Surplus-value thus appears to arise from advances as such: 'In its assumed capacity of offspring of the aggregate advanced capital, surplus-value takes the converted form of profit.'[3]

Marx also presents the mistaken idea that profit arises from capital advanced as an instance of confusion in the minds of those engaged in production between 'cost price' (constant plus variable capital) and 'real cost' (total value). Since the commodity seems to cost less than it does *in reality*, profit appears as an autonomous

[1] *Capital* Volume 3, London, 1974, p. 168.
[2] Ibid., p. 26.
[3] Ibid., p. 36.

addition to what seems to be the real cost.[4]

If values determined prices directly (that is, if commodities were exchanged on the basis of quantities of embodied labour), it would be easy to dispose of the idea that advances of capital are the source of the value over and above the cost price. Profit would be determined the moment wages were given in terms of commodities. The ratio of its magnitude to the amount of capital advanced for wages would be exactly equal to the ratio of surplus labour to necessary labour (the latter being the portion of the working day equal to the labour embodied in wage-goods). The rate of profit − the ratio of profit to total capital advanced − would then 'express nothing but what it actually is, namely a different way of measuring surplus-value, its measurement according to the value of the total capital instead of the value of the portion of capital from which surplus-value directly originates by way of its exchange for labour'.[5]

In other words, if we start from the profit contained in the price of a commodity, it is completely determined by the surplus-value contained in the value of that commodity, which is, in turn, quantitatively identical to the 'unpaid' labour over and above that required to reconstitute variable capital. The immediate determination of profits once wages are set demolishes any notion that there is an autonomous source of value other than labour.[6]

The chain of reasoning that begins with the fixing of wages and arrives at profits through the determination of the surplus labour − and therefore surplus-value − contained in commodities must be re-examined the moment prices of production (i.e., the equalization of the rate of profit) are introduced.[7] Marx introduces one further mediating factor, composed of magnitudes obtained from

[4] Ibid., p. 26. See also introduction, note 8.

[5] Ibid., p. 47.

[6] Smith had given this notion theoretical form in his concept of price as the 'addition' of autonomous components (see the introduction). We shall return to this point in the next chapter.

[7] It is opportune to note once more (see note 24 of the introduction) that Marx never based his reasoning on the assumption that the organic composition of capital is identical in all branches. In particular, in these opening pages of *Capital* Volume 3 he does not begin by positing equal organic compositions (which would guarantee an equal rate of profit on the basis of exchange at value), only to abandon the supposition later. Instead, he attempts to show that the fundamental results obtained under the assumption of exchange at value are not lost when examining exchange at prices of production.

values through the transfer of quantities of surplus-value from some capitals to others; the determination of the share of profit that goes to each capital does not conflict with the production of value and surplus-value, but simply amounts to a redistribution of total surplus-value. Once wages are set, profits are determined, because prices are merely values adjusted by the transfer of surplus-value from some capitals to others.

This is the point that must not be forgotten. The confutation of any impressions born of superficial observation of prices of production stems from the proposition that labour is the sole source of value, which Marx claims to have proved. This proposition, as we have seen, springs from another, valid for any mode of production: that labour constitutes the real social cost of products. Meanwhile, the task of scientific investigation is explicitly defined as the discovery of the forms in which the quantities of labour expended in production come to prevail in exchange.

Critical opposition to the notion that capital is a source of profit is an important aspect of this approach, which is, however, independent of and broader than this opposition itself. Marx devotes several chapters of Volume 3 to the determination of the shares of surplus-value that go to commercial capital, for he strives to uncover the origins of the price increases undergone by commodities in the sphere of distribution, and thereby to demonstrate that, contrary to the appearances of exchange relations, the labour expended in the distribution of commodities, since it produces nothing, produces no value either. This too is independent of the critique of the idea that advances of capital generate profit. Indeed, to refute that notion in no way requires any demonstration that commercial profit and the replacement of pure circulation costs arise from redistribution of industrial surplus-value.

2. Marx, Ricardo, and Prices of Production

In *Capital* Volume 1 value was defined as embodied labour. As we have seen, this is not a provisional definition. On the contrary, the law of value, which seems to be negated by the facts, actually 'asserts itself' through them as 'the rational and naturally necessary'.[8] Since

---

[8] See the letter to Kugelmann quoted in chapter 2.

prices of production diverge from values, however, the central question becomes how to explain this *difference*. Marx himself defined his own position just this way, contrasting it to that of Ricardo in some key pages of *Theories of Surplus-Value* devoted to Ricardo's theory of value.

Marx criticized the fissure in Ricardo's theory between his determination of value by embodied labour and his investigation of exchange-value: 'Ricardo's method is as follows: He begins with the determination of the magnitude of the value of the commodity by labour-time and then *examines* whether the other economic relations and categories *contradict* this determination of value or to what extent they modify it.' Such a method 'leads to erroneous results because it omits some essential links and *directly* seeks to prove the congruity of the economic categories with one another'.[9] In other words, Marx argues that Ricardo does not understand that the determination of value by labour-time is not immediately consistent with the hypothesis of a general, average rate of profit, the existence of which must 'be explained through a number of intermediary stages, a procedure which is very different from merely including it under the law of value'.[10]

We have seen that Ricardo determines value by embodied labour and have also noted his reference to a principle extraneous to the problem of exchange-values.[11] But as Sraffa has forcefully emphasized, Ricardo's theory of value is used primarily as an instrument for resolving the central problem of the determination of the rate of profit and the study of its variations consequent to changes in wages. For Ricardo, not only do exchange-values differ from ratios of embodied labour, they also vary with shifts in wages. Of the two problems – the difference between values and prices and the variation of prices with changes in wages – only the latter is important for investigation of the rate of profit. Ricardo therefore focuses attention on the study of these variations, while he presents the difference between values and prices as a 'modification' of the 'principle according to which quantity of labour expended in the production of commodities determines their relative value';

[9] *Theories of Surplus-Value*, London, 1969, Volume 2, pp. 164-65.
[10] Ibid., p. 174.
[11] See the introduction.

he does not subject it to further analysis.[12]

Marx's position is exactly the opposite: 'If Ricardo had gone into this more deeply, he would have found that − owing to the diversity in the organic composition of capital... the mere existence of a *general rate of profit* necessitates *cost-prices* that differ from *values*. ... He would also have seen how incomparably more important and decisive the understanding of this difference is for the whole theory than his observations on the variation in cost-prices of commodities brought about by the rise or fall of wages.'[13] In other words, for Marx it is not simply a matter of determining the rate of profit and production prices, but also of establishing the consequences 'for the whole theory' of the difference between values and prices. Prices must not be simply 'neutralized' as Ricardo attempts, but their deviation from values must be analysed, to see whether there is a contradiction between prices and the basis on which value is determined. Or rather, it must be shown that this contradiction is only apparent.

But Ricardo, Marx writes, deserves credit for having stated the problem definitively: 'The basis, the starting-point for the physiology of the bourgeois system − for the understanding of its internal organic coherence and life process − is the determination of *value by labour-time*. Ricardo starts with this and forces science to get out of the rut, to render an account of the extent to which the other categories − the relations of production and commerce − evolved and described by it, correspond to or contradict this basis, this starting-point; to elucidate how far a science which in fact only reflects and reproduces the manifest forms of the process, and therefore also how far these manifestations themselves, correspond to the basis on which the inner coherence, the actual physiology of bourgeois society rests.... This then is Ricardo's great historical significance for science.'[14]

---

[12] See the title of section IV of chapter I of Ricardo's *On the Principles of Political Economy and Taxation*, in *Works and Correspondence of David Ricardo*, Volume 1, Cambridge, 1951. In the next chapter we will return to this point, and in particular to Sraffa's introduction to the *Principles*.

[13] *Theories of Surplus-Value*, Volume 2, pp. 175-6. The expression 'cost-price' in the English text translates *Kostenpreis*, which Marx uses to mean 'price of production'; the passage must be interpreted accordingly. The formulation 'cost-price' is also found in the English edition of *Capital* Volume 3 as the translation of *Kostpreis*, which in this case denotes the sum of constant and variable capital. In *Capital* Marx uses 'Produktionspreis' for 'price of production'.

[14] Ibid., p. 166.

3. Prices as Absolutes: the 'Conservation of Energy'

Let us turn now to the application of Marx's approach, and more particularly to the actual functioning of the concept of the redistribution of surplus-value.

We shall set out the content of chapter 9 of *Capital* Volume 3 according to the simplest possible schema. To begin with, let us assume that no fixed capital is employed in production: constant capital will therefore consist exclusively of circulating capital. Let us further assume that our system is composed of just two industries. Now, consider one unit of each of the two commodities. Their values, denoted by μ_1 and μ_2, can be broken down into constant capital, variable captial, and surplus-value:

$$\mu_1 = c_1 + v_1 + s_1$$
$$\mu_2 = c_2 + v_2 + s_2$$

Let us further assume that the working day and the daily wage are equal in the two industries; this means that: $\frac{s_1}{v_1} = \frac{s_2}{v_2}$, in other words, the rates of surplus-value are equal.

If the two commodities are exchanged directly according to their values, then the rates of profit in the two industries may be denoted as follows:

$$\pi_1 = \frac{\mu_1 - (c_1 + v_1)}{c_1 + v_1} = \frac{s_1}{c_1 + v_1}$$

$$\pi_2 = \frac{\mu_2 - (c_2 + v_2)}{c_2 + v_2} = \frac{s_2}{c_2 + v_2}$$

In other words:

$$\pi_1 = \frac{s_1}{v_1} \frac{1}{\frac{c_1}{v_1} + 1} \qquad \pi_2 = \frac{s_2}{v_2} \frac{1}{\frac{c_2}{v_2} + 1}$$

Since we have assumed that the rate of surplus-value is uniform, whether or not the two rates of profit are equal depends solely on whether the organic composition of capital is the same in both industries, in other words, whether $\frac{c_1}{v_1}$ is equal to $\frac{c_2}{v_2}$. But there is no reason to suppose that different industries – producing different use-values – will have the same organic composition of capital. In general, then, the rates of profit will be different, which amounts to saying that the commodities cannot be exchanged in accordance with the quantities of labour embodied in them. Writes Marx: 'There is no doubt, on the other hand, that aside from unessential, incidental and mutually compensating distinctions, differences in the average rate of profit in the various branches of industry do not exist in reality, and could not exist without abolishing the entire system of capitalist production. It would seem, therefore, that here the theory of value is incompatible with the real phenomena of production, and that for this reason any attempt to understand these phenomena should be given up.'[15]

The first solution to this problem advanced by Marx is as follows: 'Thus, although in selling their commodities the capitalists of the various spheres of production recover the value of the capital consumed in their production, they do not secure the surplus-value, and consequently the profit, created in their own sphere by the production of these commodities. What they secure is only as much surplus-value, and hence profit, as falls, when uniformly distributed, to the share of every aliquot part of the total social capital.'[16]

Let us denote the magnitudes relating to the total production of our two industries by capital letters corresponding to the lower-case letters used above. For example, C_1 stands for the constant capital consumed in the total production of industry 1. H_1 and H_2 will stand for the total profits of the two industries, while h_1 and h_2 will stand for profits per unit of output; π will be the general rate of profit. These last magnitudes – profits and rate of profit – are the unknowns.

The proposition of Marx that we quoted above can now be represented in our schema as follows. Profits are shares of total surplus-value distributed among the various capitals. Thus:

$$S_1 + S_2 = H_1 + H_2$$

This distribution occurs in accordance with an equal rate of profit, computed with respect to the *values of capital*. Thus:

$$H_1 = \pi(C_1 + V_1) \text{ and } H_2 = \pi(C_2 + V_2)$$

[15] *Capital* Volume 3, p. 153.
[16] Ibid., p. 158.

From which it follows that:

$$S_1 + S_2 = H_1 + H_2 = \pi(C_1 + V_1 + C_2 + V_2)$$

Hence:

$$\pi = \frac{S_1 + S_2}{C_1 + V_1 + C_2 + V_2} = \frac{S}{C + V}$$

in which:

$$S = S_1 + S_2, \quad C = C_1 + C_2, \quad V = V_1 + V_2$$

Once π has been determined, H_1 and H_2 are also determined. Then if we divide H_1 and H_2 by the number of units produced in each industry respectively, we have h_1 and h_2. Finally, the prices of production are:

$$c_1 + v_1 + h_1 \quad \text{and} \quad c_2 + v_2 + h_2.$$

It is immediately apparent that if production prices are determined in this way, not only are total profits identical to total surplus-value, but the sum of all prices also equals total value.

Marx immediately subjects this method of determining prices of production to critical analysis. Commenting on the proposition that 'the sum of the prices of production of all commodities produced in society . . . is equal to the sum of their values', he writes: 'This statement seems to conflict with the fact that under capitalist production the elements of productive capital are, as a rule, bought on the market, and that for this reason their prices include profit which has already been realized, hence, include the price of production of the respective branch of industry together with the profit contained in it, so that the profit of one branch of industry goes into the cost-price of another. *But if we place the sum of the cost-prices of the commodities of an entire country on one side, and the sum of its surplus-values, or profits, on the other, the calculation must evidently be right.*'[17]

From the passages immediately following this point, it appears that Marx had in mind primarily the possibility that the profit contained in a certain price might be counted more than once

[17] Ibid., p. 160, emphasis added.

because it might enter into the cost-price of another commodity.[18] But he quickly comes to the real problem, which arises from the fact that 'the elements of productive capital are, as a rule, bought on the market'. This is what he means: 'Aside from the fact that the price of a particular product, let us say that of capital B, differs from its value because the surplus-value realized in B may be greater or smaller than the profit added to the price of the products of B, the same circumstance applies also to those commodities which form the constant part of capital B, and indirectly also its variable part, as the labourers' necessities of life.'[19]

In other words, Marx acknowledges here that the magnitudes on the basis of which surplus-value has been redistributed – that is, capital advanced, measured in value – are not identical to the prices at which the elements of capital are bought on the market. He therefore admits that the prices previously calculated must be adjusted. But he does assert that total value is identical to the sum of all prices. Indeed, referring to the previously quoted statement, he writes: 'However, this always resolves itself to one commodity receiving too little of the surplus-value while another receives too much, so that the deviations from the value which are embodied in the prices of production compensate one another.'[20] A few lines further on, he returns to the same point: 'It is necessary to remember this modified significance of the cost-price, and to bear in mind that there is always the possibility of an error if the cost-price of a commodity in any particular sphere is identified with the value of the means of production consumed by it. Our present analysis does not necessitate a closer examination of this point'.[21] He then discusses the resulting change in the meaning of the statement that cost-price is less than value, and concludes that, while this statement is 'modified in the individual spheres of production, the fundamental fact always remains that in the case of the total social capital the cost-price of the

---

[18] Ibid., pp. 160-1.

[19] Ibid., p. 161.

[20] Ibid., p. 161. This passage is part of the discussion that opens with the observation quoted above: 'This statement [that the sum of the prices of production of all commodities is equal to the sum of the values of these commodities] seems to conflict', etc. It is clearly intended to reply negatively to the doubt implicit in the statement. Another negative reply is given immediately after the observation expressing the doubt: see the passage located in note 17 above.

[21] Ibid., p. 165.

commodities produced by it is smaller than their value, or, in the case of the total mass of social commodities, smaller than their price of production, which is identical with their value'.[22]

Here again Marx acknowledges that errors result if prices of production are determined through the redistribution of surplus-value on the basis of capital-values advanced. He proposes no correct method of determining prices of production, but asserts that such a correction would not contradict the proposition that the sum of all prices of production is equal to total value.

On the other hand, there can be no doubt that Marx maintained that total profits always equalled total surplus-value and that total values always equalled the sum of all prices. There were difficulties (never resolved) in the case of individual prices of production, and even in the price of aggregate production (which, Marx held, could be identified with value, even in the absence of a solution to the problem of how to correct prices of production); but the assertion that profits are redistributed surplus-value presented no difficulties for Marx. In chapter 10 of *Capital* Volume 3 − in other words, after the discussion of the difficulties cited here −Marx states: 'It is evident that the average profit can be nothing but the total mass of surplus-values allotted to the various quantities of capital proportionally to their magnitudes in the different spheres of production.'[23]

Before analysing all this material, however, we must make one additional point. The prices of production obtained from the redistribution of surplus-value, calculated on the basis of capital-values advanced, are quantities of labour which originate in the movement of quantities of surplus-value from certain commodities to others. Just as values are first determined as absolute quantities based on methods of production and are later expressed in terms of a particular commodity (money), so prices of production are first obtained as absolute magnitudes − quantities of labour − and later expressed in money terms. The idea that prices of production are quantities of labour is the only really crucial point in chapter 9 and the three subsequent chapters, whereas the expression of prices of production in money appears thoroughly insignificant.

The equalities set out by Marx − total profit and total surplus-

[22] Ibid.
[23] Ibid., p. 174.

value, the sum of all prices and total value – can be challenged from two different angles. First, when we consider prices of production as quantities of labour determined by the redistribution of surplus-value on the basis of capital-values, the components of capital are handled not in terms of their prices but in terms of their values. A correction is therefore necessary, and it may be asked whether the aggregate equalities survive this correction. This is the problem we have just noted above. Second, even if we accept those prices – and thus ignore the difficulties previously noted – and if we express prices and values in money terms, it certainly does not follow automatically that the sum of all prices will equal total value, for this will depend on the organic composition of capital in the industry that produces gold.[24]

In these chapters of *Capital* Marx consistently adopts the first of these two standpoints; he never considers the question that is immediately raised if the second is adopted. It therefore seems reasonable to assume that he holds that the two equalities (total surplus-value and profit, the value and price of total production) are valid in terms of quantities of embodied labour, this being the substance of which both values and prices of production consist. Now, the reference during the discussion of these equalities to the expression of prices of production in money terms[25] would render these equalities inherently invalid, even if the prices of production obtained were correct. The explanation for this probably lies in Marx's having paid insufficient attention to this point while concentrating on the first of these two approaches and neglecting the second. The following discussion of Marx's prices of production (both in their initial determination and in the subsequent correction) will therefore refer to absolute magnitudes, namely quantities of embodied labour.

Let us now re-examine the critical analysis to which Marx subjects his own method of determining prices. As we have seen, he states explicitly that a correction is necessary. While he does not indicate precisely how this should be done, he is nevertheless clearly convinced that it is feasible and indicates the main feature of the result:

[24] See section iii of the appendix to this chapter and the following section as well.

[25] For example, pp. 159 and 173, *Capital* Volume 3. That the prices of production Marx obtains through the transformation must be understood as absolute magnitudes has been solidly established by F. Vianello, *Valori, prezzi e distribuzione del reddito*, Rome, 1970, p. 101 n.

total profit is total surplus-value redistributed, and total value equals the sum of all prices. We can develop the argument in the direction indicated by the first of Marx's determinations of prices, although this will merely illustrate Marx's idea that the result must be of this character.

The transformation may be viewed as the outcome of a series of operations. The first step is to redistribute surplus-value as profits on the basis of capital-values advanced. This gives us absolute magnitudes the sum of which still equals the total quantity of value. These magnitudes, however, cannot be considered actual prices of production because of the error Marx points to, namely the difference that would then arise between cost-prices measured in value and cost-prices measured in the prices obtained through this procedure. The mass of surplus-value must therefore be redistributed again on the basis of cost-prices measured in 'first approximation' prices.[26] But exactly the same problem arises again. Surplus-value must therefore be redistributed yet again. Since such a procedure — assuming it eventually arrives at a definite result — gives rise to absolute magnitudes obtained by the manipulation of quantities of embodied labour, the problem Marx poses indeed makes sense (if we leave aside the commodity in terms of which values and prices are expressed). The problem is whether or not, once the correction has been completed, the sum of the prices of all commodities produced is actually equal to the sum of their values.

To continue our analysis of Marx's idea, let us compare this conservation of total value to the conservation of energy in an isolated physical system.[27] Consider a simple example: a system in which *n* spherical bodies move in a gravitational field inside an airless box. For the sake of simplicity, assume that when the bodies collide with each other or with the sides of the box, they rebound in a perfectly elastic manner. Once the positions and velocities of the bodies at a particular time are known, the evolution of the system can be predicted. At time zero each body possesses a given amount of energy, part kinetic, part potential. One second later, the system has undergone a 'transformation': the energy of each individual body is, as a rule, different from what it was a second earlier and is

---

[26] This term can legitimately be used in this context. Section 4 of chapter 2 examines the illegitimate notion of value as a first approximation.

[27] The analogy is developed more fully in note 28.

differently distributed between kinetic and potential energy. But the total energy, the sum of the energy of all the individual bodies, has been conserved.

The analogy lies in the fact that the operation by which Marx passes from values to prices must also conserve a sum of quantities associated with the 'initial position', in this case the sum of values. There is, however, a decisive difference: Marx's transformation must conserve not only total value, but also its distribution between capital-value and surplus-value. It is as if, to return to the original example, not only total energy but also total kinetic energy had to be conserved.[28]

Now, what is the significance of the twofold conservation Marx has in mind? If total surplus-value and profits were equal, and if the value of total output and the sum of all prices were also equal (once prices are properly corrected), then prices and the rate of profit could be regarded as the result solely of the redistribution of surplus-value as profits. If, on the other hand, total surplus-value were conserved but total value was not, then prices of production could not be explained solely as a redistribution of surplus-value as profits, since the appearance or disappearance of quantities of value in capital would have to be explained.

Let us return to the analogy of the spherical bodies. Here we can in

[28] It may be useful to develop the analogy further. Consider the system at a given time. Each body has both potential and kinetic energy. The former is a function of the height of the body, the latter of its velocity. So long as a body does not collide with other bodies, its total energy (potential plus kinetic) remains constant; when it rises it loses kinetic and gains potential energy, when it falls it gains kinetic and loses potential. When bodies collide with each other, kinetic energy is transferred from one to another, which causes changes in the energy of the individual bodies. That they rebound after collision shows that kinetic energy is conserved. Let us consider commodities, values, cost-prices, and surplus-values as corresponding to the bodies, their total energies, potential energies, and kinetic energies respectively, at a given time; let commodities, prices of production, cost-prices (measured in prices of production), and profits correspond to the bodies, their total energies, potential energies, and kinetic energies, respectively, at a later time. Now, Marx's idea may be cast as follows: while neither the energy/value of the individual bodies/commodities nor the relation between the two components of energy/value is conserved, the total energy/value is, on the contrary, conserved, as is its distribution between potential-energy/cost-price and kinetic-energy/surplus-value. In general, this does not hold for the system of spherical bodies. It would hold, for example, if all the initial positions and velocities lay in the plane that forms the bottom of the box (and if frictionless motion occurred there). As we shall see, Marx's idea also holds only under certain conditions, which implies a reduction in the 'degree of freedom' of the system.

fact determine the 'transformation' without assuming that energy is conserved;[29] subsequently, it can be shown that this transformation does indeed conserve total energy. In Marx's theory, on the other hand, the redistribution of surplus-value as profits permits the first step of the transformation. But the calculation is not completed; Marx merely points out that one or several corrections are required. Since he does not actually reach the final result, he specifies the essential characteristic it must have if it (and not only the 'first approximation' prices) is legitimately to be considered to have been obtained through a redistribution of surplus-value as profits.

Analogously, if we were unable to determine the motion of the bodies precisely and yet asserted that it occurred *only* through the redistribution of kinetic energy, we would be implying that it is possible actually to demonstrate that kinetic energy *and* total energy are conserved. If the latter changed, this would indicate that the conservation of kinetic energy had resulted from other causes and it would no longer make sense to talk about its redistribution among the various bodies.

It is as well to state without further ado, so as to avoid misunderstanding of these last observations, that the problems posed by the lack of conservation of the quantities of value and surplus-value can be solved not by introducing some other 'source of value' but by abandoning the very idea of a source of value to begin with. We shall return to this point in the next chapter.

When we speak of 'Marx's solution' to the problem of prices of production, we are referring, for the moment, to the idea expounded in *Capital* Volume 3 that it is possible to correct the 'first approximation' prices and that the *absolute magnitudes* obtained from the correction (in other words, the manipulation of quantities of embodied labour) can legitimately be considered the result of a redistribution of surplus-value as profits. This means that total profit and the sum of all prices of production must equal total surplus-value and the value of total production respectively. (In section 5 of this chapter, we shall contrast Marx's solution with the calculation of prices of production through a system of simultaneous equations. In part ii of the appendix we shall examine the

---

[29] Since we know with precision both motion in the gravitational field and what happens in collisions.

difficulties that arise if the solution of successive redistributions of surplus-value is accepted.)

To conclude this section let us recall what was said at the beginning of this chapter about the two aspects of Marx's double conservation. The significance of conservation is that it provides the motive for the investigation – the need to demonstrate that the law of value is confirmed as valid in the determination of prices and the rate of profit – and represents the principal theme of the research. It originates in the concept of labour as the 'substance' of value and in the proposition that given quantities of this substance are necessarily permanent.

4. Marx on the Determination of the Rate of Profit

In the preceding section we made a distinction between prices of production as absolute magnitudes derived from values and the expression of these prices in terms of money or of any other commodity. We have also maintained that Marx's aggregate equalities should be understood as valid for quantities of labour (of which both prices and values are composed). That Marx considers these equalities also valid when expressed in terms of money should be regarded as a very minor inaccuracy. But if production prices are thought of in the usual way, as magnitudes that must be expressed in terms of commodities, then the interpretation of the aggregate equalities faces the following alternative.

First, the price of production may be interpreted as a 'price' in the strict sense, as expressed in the money-commodity. On the basis of this assumption, Bortkiewicz maintains that Marx's proposition that total value equals the sum of all prices: 'would be true only if the organic composition of the capital used for production of the money-commodity, i.e. gold, behaved in a very specific manner . . . with respect to the organic composition of other forms of capital. In fact, Marx never mentions this limitation. On the contrary, he asserts the identity of total price and total value in general terms without taking careful note of the relations of production of the commodity used as a measure of value and price. This assertion is thus not only not proven but false.'[30] If we accept

[30] Bortkiewicz, 'Wertrechnung und Preisrechnung in marxschen System', *Archiv für Sozialwissenschaft und Sozialpolitik, 1906-1907*.

Bortkiewicz's own assumptions – that Marx thinks of prices of production only as magnitudes expressed in terms of gold – then Bortkiewicz is undoubtedly correct. But we must note that Marx advances no hypothesis about the organic composition of the gold-producing industry, in a context where his entire attention is focused on the problems raised by variations in the organic composition in different industries. The very absence of any such hypothesis shows that Marx first conceived of aggregate equalities between the absolute magnitudes of values and prices; this conception was subsequently broadened – in inadmissible fashion, but that is unimportant – to include the expression of these same magnitudes in gold.[31]

On the other hand, Marx's assertion that the value of total production equals the sum of all prices, like his claim that the sum of profits equals the sum of surplus-value, may be conceived as implying the choice of a unit of measurement for prices. This unit is the composite commodity in which the various commodities are contained in precisely the proportions they constitute in total production, but in quantities such that one unit of the composite commodity embodies one unit of labour.[32] Then, if we replace total

[31] Dobb connects this attribution to Marx of a hypothesis about the gold-producing industry to Bortkiewicz's interpretation of the equality of total value and price. In another context, Dobb has also attributed a further hypothesis to Marx – that the organic composition of the totality of industries producing wage-goods is equal, or approximately equal, to the organic composition of social capital. There is, however, no textual basis for either of these hypotheses in Marx – unless one holds that the hypothesis on the organic composition in the gold-producing industry is implicit in the passages cited in note 25 above. In that case, however, it would be difficult to explain why Marx found this plausible or why he never discussed it explicitly, despite numerous opportunities. For the hypothesis about the gold industry, see Dobb, 'An Epoch-making Book', in *Labour Monthly*, October 1961, pp. 487-91. For the hypothesis about wage-goods, see Dobb, *Political Economy and Capitalism*, London, 1940, chapter III, paragraph 14; also R. Meek, 'Some Notes on the Transformation Problem', in *Economic Journal*, 1956, pp. 94-107. As we shall see in section iii of the appendix to this chapter, when prices are calculated properly, these hypotheses about the organic compositions of particular industries generally do not lead to the results that might be expected when considering the first-approximation prices calculated by Marx.

[32] If we adopt this unit of measurement, then the sum of prices expressed in it equals the sum of values expressed in it. These sums (which are quantities of the commodity selected as a measure) have the same numerical value as the labour embodied in total production. In his *Theory of Capitalist Development*, London, 1942 (chapter VII, section 3), Sweezy introduces this equality to render determinate the system of

output by surplus-product (total production minus the material components of constant and variable capital), we obtain the unit of measurement implicit in the equality of the sum of profits and total surplus-value.

Now, either of these two equalities, taken in itself, would be quite harmless, rather like adopting a hundredweight of grain as a unit of measurement. There would be no sense in maintaining that anything in particular is conserved in the transition from values to prices of production on the basis of just one of these equalities.[33] But there can be no doubt that Marx conceives of the two equalities as simultaneously valid, even when he presents them separately. Nor – and this is what is most important – does Marx ever present either of them as dependent on (or equivalent to) the choice of a unit for the measurement of prices. Indeed, the problem of such a unit is not even posed. As we have seen, this accords with the idea that prices are quantities of labour, shares of the labour embodied in all the commodities produced.

It is perhaps appropriate, in order to further clarify the issue, to point out that the following three propositions are equivalent:

1. The rate of profit of the system is $\dfrac{S}{C + V}$.

2. Total profit equals total surplus-value, *and* the sum of the prices of all commodities is identical to the sum of their values.

3. Total profit equals total surplus-value, *and* the sum of capital-values equals the figure obtained if cost prices are calculated by prices of production.

Even if these equalities hold – which is not generally the case, as we shall see in the following section – the equation $\dfrac{S}{V} = \dfrac{H}{W}$ (where H is the amount of profit and W is the quantity of wages paid, calculated in the production prices of wage-goods) does not necessarily follow; in other words, the rate of surplus-value is not necessarily invariable.

simultaneous equations of prices; he then ascribes this significance to the same identity in Marx. Subsequently, he replaces the implicit unit of measurement with a quantity of gold.

[33] We shall return to these aggregate equalities in the next chapter, in discussing the 'transformation problem'. We shall soon see that if prices of production are calculated directly, the two aggregate equalities cannot be satisfied simultaneously. With hindsight, it is clear that Marx's system contains two, generally incompatible units of measure. But while this may be formally true, it hinders more than helps an understanding of the transformation Marx had in mind.

If it were, and if the first equality were also valid, the organic composition would be invariable too. In the next section we shall construct an example in which equality 1 holds but the rate of surplus-value is not invariable; it should also be noted that the invariability of the latter is not at all essential to Marx's idea that profit is redistributed surplus-value: since prices and values differ, the relationship between total surplus-value and that portion of capital-value constituted by the value of labour-power need not remain invariable through the transformation of values into prices any more than the relationship between total surplus-value and, say, the value of the total quantity of steel employed need so remain.[34] Indeed, from the standpoint of the price of production, labour-power is a means of production like any other.

Although the idea that profit is redistributed surplus-value — which, as we have seen, implies that the rate of profit equals $\frac{S}{C + V}$ — does not mean that the relationship $\frac{S}{V}$ is invariable, these latter considerations, which show that no such contention is necessary, bring us close to an understanding of why Marx was wrong to believe that even the ratio $\frac{S}{C + V}$ was invariable. Indeed, as we shall soon see, to maintain that any of the ratios $\frac{S}{C + V}$, $\frac{S}{V}$, or $\frac{C}{V}$ is invariable requires either special assumptions about the composition of at least two of the aggregates total output (whose value is $C + V + S$), total wage-goods (V), and the total capital advanced ($C + V$), or special hypotheses about methods of production, or a combination of both.

5. The Determination of the Rate of Profit by a System of Simultaneous Equations

Let us now compare Marx's solution with the simultaneous calcula-tion of the rate of profit and prices of production. (By 'Marx's

---

[34] In his examination of the fall of the rate of profit in *Capital* Volume 3, Marx analyses the movement of the magnitudes $\frac{S}{V}$ and $\frac{C}{V}$ separately. These two magnitudes do not remain invariable during the transition from values to prices. Marx does main-tain, however, that the product $(\frac{S}{V})(1 + \frac{C}{V})^{-1}$ is invariable and is precisely the rate of profit, based on the idea that profit is redistributed surplus-value.

solution' we mean the contention that the rate of profit of the system equals $\dfrac{S}{C + V}$. This is both necessary and sufficient if profit is to be considered redistributed surplus-value, regardless of how prices are obtained, and especially when they are not determined as absolute quantities. Indeed, if the rate of profit were $\dfrac{S}{C + V}$, then the statement that $H = S$ would imply that the sum of all prices equalled the value of total output.)

To begin with, we must re-examine the magnitudes of value we used in the previous section. These can be determined only from the quantities characteristic of the prevalent methods of production. Let us continue to assume that the system is composed of only two industries, and let us again select the simplest possible example: industry 1 produces the sole means of production of the system, using a_1 units of commodity 1 itself for each unit produced. Industry 2 uses a_2 units of commodity 1 for each unit produced. Let the quantities of labour directly required per unit produced be m_1 and m_2 respectively. We can now calculate the quantity of embodied labour in one unit of commodity 1: it can be obtained by solving the equation $\mu_1 = m_1 + a_1\mu_1$. The magnitude thus obtained can then be used to calculate the quantity of labour embodied in one unit of commodity 2: $\mu_2 = m_2 + a_2\mu_1$.

Let us now assume that wages, expressed in physical terms, consist of f units of commodity 1 for each unit of labour (commodity 2 is therefore a 'luxury good'); finally, let q_1 and q_2 equal the quantities of the two commodities produced. On the basis of the given methods of production, using the quantities of embodied labour we have calculated, we can now compute all the magnitudes implied in Marx's calculation of prices of production (for example: $c_1 = a_1\mu_1$, $C_1 = q_1c_1$). It need only be added that, for the system to be able to turn out a net product, a_1 must be less than 1, and if there is to be surplus-value and profit, the quantity $a_1 + m_1f$ must also be less than 1.

We may now compare the rate of profit as formulated by Marx with that obtained through a simultaneous calculation of prices and the rate of profit. The system of prices of production is as follows:

$$p_1 = (a_1p_1 + m_1w)(1 + r)$$
$$p_2 = (a_2p_1 + m_2w)(1 + r)$$
$$w = fp_1$$

in which p_1 and p_2 denote the prices of commodities, r is the rate of profit and w the wage rate. If we insert the third equation into the first two, we obtain:

$$p_1 = (a_1 p_1 + m_1 f p_1)(1 + r)$$
$$p_2 = (a_2 p_1 + m_2 f p_1)(1 + r).$$

The choice of a unit of measurement for prices completes the system, giving us as many equations as there are unknowns.

The first equation alone determines the rate of profit. This is to be expected, since the first industry produces a commodity by means of that commodity alone: both means of production and wages are composed of commodity 1; r is therefore equal to the surplus product of the first industry divided by the capital advanced, which is physically homogeneous with the surplus product:

$$r = \frac{1 - (a + m_1 f)}{a + m_1 f}$$

Let us now return to Marx's formula, rewriting it to highlight its salient characteristics:

$$\pi = \frac{S}{C + V} = \frac{S_1 + S_2}{C_1 + V_1 + C_2 + V_2}$$

$$= \frac{\frac{S_1}{C_1 + V_1}(C_1 + V_1) + \frac{S_2}{C_2 + V_2}(C_2 + V_2)}{(C_1 + V_1) + (C_2 + V_2)}$$

$$= \frac{\pi_1(C_1 + V_1) + \pi_2(C_2 + V_2)}{(C_1 + V_1) + (C_2 + V_2)} = \frac{\pi_1(c_1 + v_1)q_1 + \pi_2(c_2 + v_2)q_2}{(c_1 + v_1)q_1 + (c_2 + v_2)q_2}$$

In Marx's formula, then, the rate of profit is the weighted mean of the individual rates of profit of the two industries, the weights being represented by the capital-values advanced. These in turn depend on the quantities produced in the industries. In our example:

$$\pi_1 = \frac{S_1}{C_1 + V_1} = \frac{\mu_1 - (a_1\mu_1 + mf\mu_1)}{a_1\mu_1 + mf\mu_1} = \frac{1 - (a_1 + m_1 f)}{a_1 + m_1 f} = r$$

whereas π_2 will as a rule be a different magnitude. The figure π will therefore fall between π_1 and π_2 and will coincide with r; in other words, it will coincide with the actual rate of profit only if $q_2 = 0$.

More generally, if the system is composed of a large number of industries, and if wages are physically determined by the subsistence goods required to reproduce labour-power, then the rate of profit is determined in that part of the system made up of industries directly or indirectly producing wage-goods; the prices for the remaining industries are adjusted on the basis of the prices and rate of profit calculated in this part of the system. The rate of profit as calculated by Marx coincides with the actual rate only under certain conditions, for example: 1. if the organic composition of capital is equal in the various industries; 2. if the composition of total output is identical to the composition of the aggregate of commodities, both means of production and wage goods, that must be advanced to obtain that output.[35]

The first case is self-evident, since commodities are exchanged in accordance with their values. In the second case, although production prices will generally differ from values, the identical composition of the surplus product and the aggregate capital advanced means that the rate of profit will be the same whether calculated on the basis of prices or values.

As has already been pointed out, the equation $r = \pi$ – in other words, the invariability of the relation $\dfrac{S}{C + V}$ in the transition from values to prices – does not imply that $\dfrac{S}{V}$ (or, therefore, $\dfrac{C}{V}$) is invariable. Consider a system composed of just two commodities, a means of production and a wage-good, and assume that case 2 obtains, in other words, that the composition of total output and of total advances is identical. Let γ and δ denote the quantities advanced of means of production and wage-goods respectively. We then have $\dfrac{C}{V} = \dfrac{\gamma u_1}{\delta u_2}$, while the same ratio, measured in prices of production, is $\dfrac{\gamma p_1}{\delta p_2}$ (commodity 1 being the means of production, commodity 2 the wage-good). These two magnitudes are equal if and only if $\dfrac{u_1}{u_2} = \dfrac{p_1}{p_2}$. But if, as is generally the case, $\dfrac{u_1}{u_2} \neq \dfrac{p_1}{p_2}$, then since $\dfrac{H}{C' + W} = \dfrac{S}{C + V}$ (where C' is the aggregate of the means of production measured in prices), and $\dfrac{C'}{W} \neq \dfrac{C}{V}$, then $\dfrac{H}{W} \neq \dfrac{S}{V}$. (The equality of

---

[35] For a more detailed analysis of this point, see section i of the appendix to this chapter.

$\frac{H}{W}$ and $\frac{S}{V}$ would be assured, on the other hand, if the composition of the net product equalled the composition of the aggregates of wage-goods, regardless of whether r equalled π.)

In sum, then, we may conclude that unless the methods of production and/or the composition of output are exceptional, the actual rate of profit is not the same as the rate calculated by Marx. From which it follows that profits cannot be considered the result of a redistribution of total surplus-value.

6. Price Formation and Commercial Capital

The whole of *Capital* Volume 3 is dominated by the idea that prices are formed by the redistribution of total surplus-value. We shall not dwell on absolute rent, except to note that Marx holds that it arises from the exclusion of the surplus-value produced in agriculture from this redistribution, a consequence of the monopoly of power of the landowning class. Let us return, however, to commercial capital. The exclusion of circulation costs from value must be confirmed through the determination of prices. It must therefore be shown that the general rate of profit, the magnitude that appears on the surface, is formed, once commercial capital is included, by a uniform distribution, in proportion to capital advances, of the surplus-value produced in the 'industrial sector'.

Let us again examine the simplest possible example.[36] To avoid all complications, we shall assume that production occurs through direct labour alone, without constant capital, and that the same is true for circulation. The advances of the commercial and industrial capitalists therefore consist solely of wages. (In reality, of course, the commercial capitalists must advance not only the wages of the workers employed in distribution, but also – at least – the value of the commodities they subsequently resell; but it is pointless to complicate this simple illustration of Marx's idea by introducing differences in 'organic composition'.[37] We shall therefore assume

[36] See *Capital* Volume 3, chapter 17.

[37] The organic composition in industry is zero; but the organic composition in commerce, if we use that term to refer to the ratio between non-wage and wage advances, would be positive, because of the advances needed to buy commodities for subsequent resale.

that commercial capitalists calculate the rate of profit on the basis of distribution costs alone.)

Let L be the value of the social product, i.e. the labour necessary to *produce* the commodities, and M be the labour expended in circulation. Let w be the value of one unit of labour-power, i.e. the labour embodied in the wage-goods required to reproduce that unit. The surplus-value produced is then $L - Lw$. But a portion of this must replace the commercial capitalists' expenditure on wages, which amounts to Mw. Total profit is therefore $L - (L + M)w$ and is distributed uniformly between industrial and commercial capitalists. The rate of profit is obtained by dividing the profit, i.e. the surplus-value that remains available for distribution, by the total capital advanced, which is composed of capital advanced in production plus that advanced in circulation. The rate of profit, then, is:

$$\pi = \frac{L - (L + M)w}{(L + M)w}.$$

Prices are formed on the basis of the rate of profit calculated in this way. For a given commodity, let λ be the labour embodied and μ the labour expended in circulation. The 'wholesale' price is then $\lambda w(1 + \pi)$; after circulation, the price is:

$$\lambda w(1 + \pi) + \mu w(1 + \pi) = (\lambda + \mu)\, w(1 + \pi)$$

$$= \frac{\lambda + \mu}{L + M}\, L.$$

For the aggregate of commodities,[38] the wholesale price is $Lw(1 + \pi)$, and the final price $Lw(1 + \pi) + Mw(1 + \pi) = L$.

There now arises a problem similar to that posed by the transformation presented in chapter 9 of *Capital* Volume 3. Labour-power has both a value and a price. The value of a unit of labour-power is the labour embodied in the wage-goods required to reproduce this unit; let it be denoted by w. Let z be the labour required for the circulation of this aggregate of commodities. Its price is $\frac{w + z}{L + M}\, L$, which coincides with w only if $\frac{w}{z} = \frac{L}{M}$, that is, if the labour embodied

---

[38] Wholesale prices are lower than values. The difference, $L + - Lw(1 + \pi) = Mw(1 + \pi)$, goes to the commercial capitalists. This is exactly what Marx has in mind. See *Capital* Volume 3, p. 293.

in the aggregate of wage-goods stands in the same ratio to the labour required for the circulation of wage-goods as L does to M.

If we make this assumption, then the rate of profit and the prices calculated by Marx's method are correct. To see this it is sufficient to calculate the rate of profit directly. Let w' be the price of a unit of labour-power (no matter how measured), and r be the rate of profit. The price of wage-goods per unit of labour-power *is $ww'(1 + r) + zw'(1 + r)$*, which must equal w'. It follows that $r = \dfrac{1 - (w + z)}{(w + z)}$. But since $z = \dfrac{M}{L}w$, we have: $r = \dfrac{L - (L + M)w}{(L + M)w} = \pi$. It follows at once that directly calculated prices correspond to those calculated by Marx's method.

But once we abandon this assumption about the ratio between circulation costs and the production costs of wage-goods, the simultaneous calculation of prices and the rate of profit turns out differently. As in the example presented in section 5 above, the simultaneously calculated rate of profit is unaffected by what happens outside the production – and in this case circulation – of wage-goods. Under Marx's method of calculation, by contrast, all sectors of the system influence the rate of profit. We must therefore conclude that the profit that accrues to the commercial sector and the recovery of capital advanced for pure circulation costs cannot be strictly considered deductions from the surplus-value produced in the industrial sector.

What we have seen so far is sufficient to illustrate the difficulties of Marx's idea. And of course, if we abandon both the hypothesis that no constant capital is involved and the simplification concerning the capital advances of commercial capitalists, these difficulties are compounded by those arising from the differing organic compositions.[39]

7. The Impasse of Marx's Project

As we have seen, Marx himself was the first critic of transformation

[39] J. Harrison, 'Productive and Unproductive Labour in Marx's Political Economy', in *Bulletin of the Conference of Socialist Economists*, 1973, pp. 77-78, argues that problems arise only from the failure to make a clear distinction between commercial and industrial capital. But even if such a distinction is made and the simplest hypotheses imaginable maintained, Marx's idea remains untenable.

through the redistribution of surplus-value on the basis of capital-values advanced. He did maintain, however, that the necessary correction for prices of production would not affect the conservation of aggregate quantities.

On the one hand, prices must ultimately be reduced to quantities of labour; on the other hand, however – and this was Marx's intuitive premise – it is certainly possible to do so: the labour embodied in all the commodities produced and that portion of it which exceeds the labour required to produce the means of subsistence of the workers and replace the means of production expended in the process, cannot be altered by the distribution of profits among the capitalists.

The principle of real cost – in other words, the idea that labour constitutes the real cost of the goods produced – was already inherent in the work of Smith and Ricardo, where it implied a logic of production in general. This idea, together with the belief that the quantity of labour – the effort that has gone into the production of the goods – must be reflected in the exchange of commodities, leads to the identification of value with labour. This proposition in turn implies that an attempt must be made to reduce actual exchange-values to labour. The formation of prices, as regards both the uniform distribution of profit and the determination of commercial profit, can then be considered the effect of a redistribution of total surplus-value as profits. The propositions that underlie the theory can thus be confirmed by analysis of actual phenomena, which can be shown to conform to the essence of the theory, even if not immediately.

Understood in this strict sense, Marx's approach encounters an insuperable obstacle in the determination of prices. In the following two chapters we shall consider whether it is possible to enumerate aspects of Marx's investigation that can be disengaged from the labour theory of value.

Appendices

(i) Further on Marx's formula for the rate of profit

Let us return to the conditions under which the actual rate of profit corresponds to that calculated according to Marx's method.[40] We will consider a system composed of *n* industries. Let:

$q = [q_1, q_2, \ldots, q_n]$ be the row vector of the quantities produced;

$$m = \begin{bmatrix} m_1 \\ m_2 \\ \vdots \\ m_n \end{bmatrix}$$ the column vector of the quantities of labour directly required per unit of output;

$A = [a_{ik}]$, where a_{ik} is the quantity of the commodity *k* consumed as means of production in industry *i* per unit of output;

$f = [f_1, f_2, \ldots f_n]$, the quantities of means of subsistence that determine the wage per unit of labour-power;

$F = mf = [m_i f_k]$;

$B = A + F = [a_{ik} + m_i f_k]$;

p the column vector of prices of production;

r the rate of profit;

w the wage per unit of labour-power.

Let us assume that *q* satisfies the condition $qB \leqslant q$ (in other words, no component of *qB* is greater than the corresponding component of *q*, and at least one is smaller).

The system of prices of production is:

$$(Ap + mw)(1 + r) = p$$
$$w = fp$$

Inserting the expression for *w* into the first equation:

$$Bp(1 + r) = p$$

If we arrange the industries so that those producing wage-goods, whether directly or indirectly, appear first, the matrix *B* assumes the form:

$$B = \begin{bmatrix} B_{11} & 0 \\ B_{21} & B_{22} \end{bmatrix}$$

where B_{11} and B_{22} are square and B_{11} is irreducible. The commodities of the system produced by the industries represented by B_{11} are

[40] This appendix assumes a detailed knowledge of Sraffa's *Production of Commodities by Means of Commodities* and some knowledge of the elements of the theory of positive matrices.

basic commodities as defined by Sraffa, wage-goods being included in the means of production.[41] All the commodities of this first group enter, directly or indirectly, into all the others, whether of the first or second groups, at least through the wage-goods; non-zero elements thus appear in each row of B_{21}. Let us further assume that the standard ratio[42] of matrix B_{11} is smaller than that of B_{22}.

If we denote the vector of the prices of the basic commodities by p_1 and of the non-basic ones by p_2, the system may be written thus:

$$B_{11}p_1(1 + r) = p_1$$
$$B_{21}p_1(1 + r) + B_{22}p_2(1 + r) = p_2$$

The rate of profit is determined solely by the system of basic commodities and is equal to the standard ratio of that system. If we insert p_1 and r into the second group of equations, we get p_2, which is positive by virtue of our assumption about the standard ratios of the two groups of commodities.

Let us now make the calculation by Marx's method. $\mu = (I - A)^{-1}m$ is the vector of the quantities of embodied labour. The rate of profit is:

$$\pi = \frac{S}{C + V} = \frac{(C + V + S) - (C + V)}{C + V} = \frac{q\mu - qB\mu}{qB\mu}$$

This is dependent on the entire matrix B and not only on B_{11}. The equality $\pi = r$ implies that

$$q\mu - qB\mu = rqB\mu$$

that is:

$$q[I - (1 + r)B]\mu = 0$$

Let us look at two cases in which this condition is satisfied.

In the first:

$$q[I - (1 + r)B] = 0$$

[41] *Production of Commodities by Means of Commodities*, Cambridge, 1960, p. 8.

[42] Sraffa uses the terms 'Standard System' and 'Standard Ratio', referring to a system in which wage-goods are not part of the totality of means of production. But there is no difficulty in extending the use of such ideas to a system in which the surplus consists entirely of profits.

In this case the real system coincides with its associated standard system. In the second:

$$[I - (1 + r)B]\mu = 0$$

In this case $\mu = (1 + r)A\mu + (1 + r)F\mu$, from which $\mu_i = c_i + v_i + s_i = (1 + r)c_i + (1 + r)v_i$. Therefore, $s_i = r(c_i + v_i)$, that is: $r = \dfrac{s_i}{c_i + v_i} = \pi_i$. All the individual rates of profit, and hence the organic compositions, are equal.

These are not the only cases in which r can equal π. There are others which produce the 'compensations' Marx had in mind. Let us confect an example in which neither of the two conditions above are satisfied and yet r is still equal to π.

Assume that there are three commodities, all of them basic. Let $q^* = [q_1^*, q_2^*, q_3^*]$ be the left-hand eigenvector of B associated with the eigenvalue $\dfrac{1}{1 + r}$. The composition of q^* is that of the standard commodity of the system. In the standard system — the imaginary system in which q^* was the vector of the quantities produced, A the matrix of the quantities used per unit of output, etc. — we would have, under condition 1:

$$r = \pi = \frac{\pi_1(c_1 + v_1)q_1^* + \pi_2(c_2 + v_2)q_2^* + \pi_3(c_3 + v_3)q_3^*}{(c_1 + v_1)q_1^* + (c_2 + v_2)q_2^* + (c_3 + v_3)q_3^*}$$

Let us assume that the quantities produced in the real system are

$$q = \left[q_1^* + \alpha, q_2^*, q_3^* - \alpha \frac{(c_1 + v_1)(\pi_1 - r)}{(c_3 + v_3)(\pi_3 - r)}\right]$$

where α is greater than zero but sufficiently small that $qB \leqslant q$, which is always possible since $q^*B < q^*$. It is easy to show that $r = \pi$ holds in the real system as well.

The whole question of the equality of r and π can be usefully restated in geometric terms. Let us assume, for the sake of simplicity, that B is irreducible. The set of vectors q such that $qB \leqslant q$, $q > 0$, is a cone, which we shall call Q, contained in the cone of vectors having no negative components. While r depends only on B, π, the rate of profit as calculated by Marx, is a function of q:

$$\pi(q) = \frac{\overset{n}{\underset{k=1}{\Sigma}} \pi_k(c_k + v_k)q_k}{\overset{n}{\underset{k=1}{\Sigma}} (c_k + v_k)q_k}$$

The vectors that satisfy the condition $\pi(q) = r$ are those belonging to the hyper-plane M, the equation of which is:

$$r \overset{n}{\underset{k=1}{\Sigma}} (c_k + v_k)q_k = \overset{n}{\underset{k=1}{\Sigma}} \pi_k(c_k + v_k)q_k.$$

The intersection of M and Q is never empty because it contains at least the vectors of the line T, of equation $q = \tau q^*$ (where q^* is the vector representing the standard system). Since $q^*B = \frac{1}{1+r} q^* < q^*$, q* lies within the cone Q. The intersection of Q and M is therefore a space of dimension $n - 1$, contained in Q. If $n = 2$, this intersection is reduced to the line T. It is for this reason that in constructing our example we have had to resort to a system composed of three industries. Thus, only if $n = 2$ is it generally true that $\pi = r$, if and only if the organic compositions are equal or if the system is in standard proportions. Since the set of vectors for which $\pi = r$ is of dimension one less than the cone Q, it is legitimate to assert that $r \neq \pi$, apart from exceptional cases.

By the same method we could also examine the necessary and sufficient conditions for the equalities $\frac{S}{V} = \frac{H}{W}$ and $\frac{C}{V} = \frac{C'}{W}$.

(ii)   The idea of an iterative process

The need, espoused by Marx, to correct the calculation of prices of production by considering cost-prices equal to values suggests that this calculation may be viewed as the first step in an iterative process which, beginning from values, leads by successive approximations to prices of production and the rate of profit. And indeed such a process is conceivable. Let us examine the simple system we used in section 4 of this chapter.

Using the symbols introduced in the first part of this appendix:

$$A = \begin{bmatrix} a_1 & 0 \\ a_2 & 0 \end{bmatrix}, \quad m = \begin{bmatrix} m_1 \\ m_2 \end{bmatrix}, \quad q = \begin{bmatrix} q_1, q_2 \end{bmatrix},$$

$$F = \begin{bmatrix} m_1 f & 0 \\ m_2 f & 0 \end{bmatrix}, B = \begin{bmatrix} a_1 + m_1 f & 0 \\ a_2 + m_2 f & 0 \end{bmatrix}$$

Let us now determine the 'first approximation' prices. Let π^0 denote the rate of profit and t^0 the vector of prices:

$$\pi^0 = \frac{q\mu - qB\mu}{qB\mu}, \quad t^0 = B\mu(1 + \pi^0)$$

As we know, these prices are incorrect. Let us then repeat the operation on the basis of the magnitudes obtained. Let t^1 denote the vector of new prices and π^1 the new rate of profit. Then:

$$\pi^1 = \frac{qt^0 - qBt^0}{qBt^0} = \frac{qB\mu - qB^2\mu}{qB^2\mu}$$

$$t^1 = Bt^0(1 + \pi^1) = B^2\mu(1 + \pi^0)(1 + \pi^1)$$

Continuing the iteration we obtain:

$$\pi^n = \frac{qB^n\mu - qB^{n+1}\mu}{qB^{n-1}\mu}$$

$$t^n = B^{n+1}\mu(1 + \pi^0)(1 + \pi^1) \ldots (1 + \pi^n)$$

The iterative procedure described here can be applied to any system. Under certain assumptions concerning the matrix B, π^n and t^n converge, respectively, to the rate of profit and the prices determined by the system $Bp(1 + r) = p$.[43] In this case it is sufficient to arrive at π^1 and t^1 to obtain the result. In fact, setting $c = a_1 + m_1 f$ and $d = a_2 + m_2 f$, since $\dfrac{B^k}{c^{k-1}} = B$,

$$\pi^n = \pi^{n-1} = \ldots = \pi^1 = \frac{(q_1 c + q_2 d)\mu_1 - (q_1 c^2 + q_2 cd)\mu_1}{(q_1 c^2 + q_2 cd)\mu_1} = \frac{1 - c}{c}$$

Furthermore:

$$t^n = t^{n-1} = \ldots = t^1 = B\mu(1 + \pi^0)$$

[43] H. Nikaido, *Convex Structures of Economic Theory*, New York, 1968.

Finally, if we substitute π^1 and t^1 in the equation that determines production prices and the rate of profit:

$$t^1 = B\mu(1 + \pi^0) = \frac{B^2}{c}\mu(1 + \pi^0)$$

$$= B[B\mu(1 + \pi^0)(1 + \pi^1)] = Bt^1(1 + \pi^1)$$

π^1 and t^1 are therefore solutions.

By iterating Marx's procedure we thus arrive at the correct result. But, naturally, the aggregate equalities no longer hold. Moreover, the quantities of embodied labour play no special role. As is immediately apparent, the identical result would have been obtained – and would generally be obtained even in other examples – if the starting point was, for example, the weights of the commodities, or even any other series of positive numbers.

Observing the successive steps of the iteration, it is easy to see that if total 'surplus-value' is calculated on the basis of prices t^0, obtained from values according to Marx's procedure, the result is the magnitude: $qt^0 - qBt^0$. This magnitude, exceptional cases aside, is not the same as $q\mu - qB\mu$, which is the surplus-value. In other words, what is redistributed are 'surplus values' that change continually during the procedure. The claim that the quantity of value is conserved during the iterative process is thus devoid of meaning.

(iii)   Production prices and organic compositions

For 'first approximation' production prices – that is, prices calculated by redistributing surplus-value on the basis of capital-values advanced – the following proposition holds: if the values and production prices of commodities 1 and 2 are denoted by μ_1 and μ_2 and p_1 and p_2 respectively, then:

$$\frac{p_1}{\mu_1} > \frac{p_2}{\mu_2}, \frac{p_1}{\mu_1} = \frac{p_2}{\mu_2}, \frac{p_1}{\mu_1} < \frac{p_2}{\mu_2}$$

provided that

$$\frac{c_1}{v_1} > \frac{c_2}{v_2}, \frac{c_1}{v_1} = \frac{c_2}{v_2}, \frac{c_1}{v_1} < \frac{c_2}{v_2}$$

respectively. This is immediately evident, since, if we let σ denote the rate of surplus value and ω_i the organic composition of industry i, then:

$$\frac{p_i}{\mu_i} = \frac{(c_i + v_i)(1 + \pi)}{c_i + v_i(1 + \sigma)} = \frac{(\omega_i + 1)(1 + \pi)}{\omega_i(1 + \sigma)}$$

and this is a strictly increasing function of ω_i.

If we consider the total product: $\frac{p}{\mu} = 1$. It follows that the price of a commodity is greater than, less than, or equal to its value depending on whether the organic composition of the capital that produces it is greater than, less than, or equal to the organic composition of social capital as a whole.

Moreover, if the organic composition of the industry producing gold were equal to that of total social capital, then the sum of the prices of production of the total product, as expressed in gold, would equal the sum of the values of the total product, also expressed in gold. Or, if the organic composition of the wage-good sector were equal to the organic composition of total social capital, the value and price of labour-power would be equal, as would total value and the sum of all prices, and total surplus-value and total profit too.

One thing must be stated immediately, however. The organic composition $\frac{c_i}{v_i}$ is equal to $\frac{c_i(1 + \sigma)}{m_i}$ where m_i is the quantity of labour directly necessary in industry i. Thus, for example, $\frac{c_1}{v_1} > \frac{c_2}{v_2}$ if and only if $\frac{c_1}{m_1} > \frac{c_2}{m_2}$. In other words, the proposition stated above can be reformulated, substituting $\frac{c_i}{m_i}$ for $\frac{c_i}{v_i}$; this means that the inequalities between ratios $\frac{c_i}{m_i}$ determine those between the ratios $\frac{p_i}{\mu_i}$, whatever the composition and level of wages. For example, if $\frac{c_1}{m_1} > \frac{c_2}{m_2}$ then $\frac{p_1}{\mu_1} > \frac{p_2}{\mu_2}$, however much below its maximum the wage may be.

If prices are calculated correctly, however, the proposition is no longer universally valid, as may be seen from what follows.[44]

[44] It should be noted that in referring to Marx's 'first approximation' prices, we have been dealing with absolute magnitudes. When prices are obtained from the solution of a system of simultaneous equations, they must be referred to a measure. This means that in considering relations between the magnitudes that appear in the proposition as stated, all prices should be referred to the same measure; the proposition itself, of course, is independent of the measure selected.

Let us start from the case in which the organic compositions are equal in industries 1 and 2. The proposition we must disprove is this: if $\frac{c_1}{m_1} = \frac{c_2}{m_2}$ then commodities 1 and 2 are exchanged according to the labour embodied, for every level of the wage.

Let us solve the system of production prices:

$$p = [I - A(1 + r)]^{-1} mw(1 + r)$$

If we measure in terms of 'labour commanded' and we expand the matrix

$$[I - A(1 + r)]^{-1}, p^L = m(1 + r) + Am(1 + r)^2 + \ldots$$

for p_1^L and p_2^L we shall have:

$$p_1^L = m_1(1 + r) + m_1^1(1 + r)^2 + \ldots$$
$$p_2^L = m_2(1 + r) + m_2^1(1 + r)^2 + \ldots$$

The assertion that the equality of the organic compositions implies that $\frac{p_1^L}{p_2^L} = \frac{\mu_1}{\mu_2}$ for each wage level is equivalent to the assertion that the equality

$$\frac{c_1}{m_1} = \frac{\sum\limits_{k=1}^{\infty} m_1^k}{m_1} = \frac{\sum\limits_{k=1}^{\infty} m_2^k}{m_2} = \frac{c_2}{m_2} \quad ,$$

given

$$\beta = \frac{\mu_1}{\mu_2},$$

implies:

$$m_1(1 + r) + m_1^1(1 + r)^2 + \ldots = \beta[m_2(1 + r) + m_2^1(1 + r)^2 + \ldots]$$

for all values of r such that the two series converge. On the other hand, the equality of two power series, over a complete interval of values of the variable, implies the equality of the corresponding coefficients. In this case:

$$m_1 = \beta m_2, m_1^1 = \beta m_2^1, \ldots;$$

therefore:

$$\frac{m_1{}^1}{m_1} = \frac{m_2{}^1}{m_2}, \frac{m_1{}^2}{m_1} = \frac{m_2{}^2}{m_2}, \ldots$$

In other words, if the equality of the organic compositions in industries 1 and 2 implied exchange of commodities 1 and 2 according to their values, and therefore the invariability of the ratio between their production prices, then the equality of the organic compositions would also imply the equality of the distributions in time of the dated quantities of labour. That this is not generally true can be shown immediately by the following example.

Let:

$$A = \begin{bmatrix} 0 & 0 & a \\ b & 0 & 0 \\ 0 & c & 0 \end{bmatrix}$$

We have:

$$(I - A)^{-1} = \frac{1}{1 - abc} \begin{bmatrix} 1 & ac & a \\ b & 1 & ab \\ bc & c & 1 \end{bmatrix}$$

As is easily seen, the equality of the organic compositions in industries 1 and 2 implies:

$$\frac{abcm_1 + acm_2 + am_3}{m_1} = \frac{bm_1 + abcm_2 + abm_3}{m_2}$$

If we let:

$$a = \frac{1}{2}, b = \frac{1}{3}, c = \frac{1}{4};$$

$$m_1 = m_2 = 1, m_3 = \frac{5}{8},$$

the last-mentioned equality holds, but:

$$\frac{m_1{}^1}{m_1} = \frac{am_3}{m_1} = \frac{5}{16}, \text{ whereas } \frac{m_2{}^1}{m_2} = \frac{bm_1}{m_1} = \frac{1}{3}.$$

On the basis of this example, it is now a simple matter to construct a case in which $\frac{c_1}{v_1} > \frac{c_1}{v_1}$ and $\frac{p_1{}^L}{\mu_1} < \frac{p_2{}^L}{\mu_2}$ nevertheless, or vice-versa. Let us fix a level for the rate of profit, such that, for example, $\frac{p_1{}^L}{\mu_1} < \frac{p_2{}^L}{\mu_2}$;

$p_1{}^L$, $p_2{}^L$, μ_1, and μ_2 for each given rate of profit are continuous functions of a, b, c, m_1, m_2, m_3. Let us hold all these magnitudes constant at the values previously determined, except for m_3. For the continuity mentioned, there is a neighbourhood of $\frac{5}{8}$, let us say the interval $[\frac{5}{8} - \eta, \frac{5}{8} + \eta]$ such that if m_3 remains in that interval, then $\frac{p_1{}^L}{\mu_1}$ is less than $\frac{p_2{}^L}{\mu_2}$; but as m_3 varies within that interval, we move from

$$\frac{c_1}{v_1} < \frac{c_2}{v_2} \quad \text{to} \quad \frac{c_1}{v_1} = \frac{c_2}{v_2} \quad \text{to} \quad \frac{c_1}{v_1} > \frac{c_2}{v_2}.$$

The view that the proposition stated at the beginning of section iii of this appendix is unaffected by the correct calculation of prices of production is prevalent in works on the transformation problem written before the publication of *Production of Commodities by Means of Commodities*.[45] This is exemplified by the work of Seton, who demonstrates its validity in a special case but never considers what happens in general.[46]

---

[45] For a clear explanation of the reasons why this proposition is not valid, see the example of the wine and the old oak chest (*Production of Commodities by Means of Commodities*, pp. 37-38). The organic composition in the industry producing the old oak chest is less than that of the industry producing the wine. According to the proposition in question, the price of production of an old oak chest should be, for any value of wages below the maximum, less than the price of production of a quantity of wine containing the same quantity of labour. But that this is not so is shown by the graph depicting the difference between the two prices (p. 38). It can be readily verified that Sraffa's hypothesis that wages are paid at the end of the year makes no significant difference.

[46] Seton divides the economy into three sectors, one producing means of production, the second wage-goods, the third luxury items; each sector has only one price of production. As is well known (see P. Garegnani, *Il Capitale nelle teorie della distribuzione*, Milan, pp. 51-2), it generally makes no sense to attribute only one price of production to a sector composed of a number of industries. Seton's proof *is* valid, however, if his three sectors are understood as three industries, the first of which produces the only means of production, the second the only wage-good, and the third the only luxury good.

IV

Marx and Prices of Production: the Subsequent Debate

1. 'Solutions' of the Transformation Problem

In the previous chapter, especially its first two sections, we empha-sized the distinguishing feature of Marx's investigation of prices of production. His aim was not merely to determine those prices, but to account for their divergence from values. Only if such differences offset each other – if the aggregate quantities remain the same – is the 'basis on which value is determined', which is obscured by these differences, confirmed by analysis of the prices of production.

From Bortkiewicz onwards, everyone who has attempted 'to solve' the transformation problem has invariably viewed Marx's transformation purely as an analytical expedient through which prices of production can be reached on the basis of values. They have interpreted the 'aggregate equalities' (price and value; profit and surplus, etc.) either as an unimportant aspect of this expedient or as merely a choice of *numéraire* for prices, or, finally, as a particular hypothesis about the industry producing the money-commodity. It is not our intention to present an account of these attempts, nor to go into great detail. It will be sufficient to set out the results in their definitive form and to examine them in the light of what has by now been well established: that prices of production can be determined on the basis of the production methods in each industry (i.e. the quantities of commodities produced and used in production, however they are measured) and of wages, expressed in terms of any commodity (perhaps a composite one).

Two types of 'solution' of the transformation problem can be distinguished.

1. When determining prices of production through a system of

simultaneous equations on the basis of the quantities of the various commodities produced and used, these quantities can be replaced by quantities of embodied labour. In place of a given quantity – of wheat measured in quintals, for example – the labour embodied in it can be substituted, provided, of course, that the same substitution is made every time wheat is considered, whether as a means of production or as a product. This is a particular application of the general possibility of altering the physical measure of any commodity. Naturally, the prices of production obtained on the basis of quantities of embodied labour will differ from those obtained using physical quantities measured in their 'natural' units, just as, for example, the measure of wheat in quintals differs from its measure in tons, or the measure of meat in quintals from its measure in kilos. The rate of profit, however, obviously remains unchanged.

In the final analysis, these are the main features of the attempted solutions that stand in the tradition of Bortkiewicz. It should be noted that the quantities of labour embodied in different commodities cannot legitimately be added up, any more than quintals of wheat and quintals of meat can be summed.[1] Labour therefore figures in these calculations only as a *physical measure*, and not at all as a *cost*. This, then, is an instance not of the transformation of values into prices, but of the determination of prices through one particular physical measure of commodities. The important thing is the simultaneous calculation – the quantities of labour are an otherwise useless tool.

2. On the basis of investigation of production methods, the quantities of embodied labour can be determined. These are linked, through a reversible linear relationship, to the quantities of directly necessary labour. The quantities of direct labour can then be expressed as linear functions of quantities of embodied labour. On the other hand, given the wage in physical terms, the rate of profit can be calculated. Once this is known, prices of production can be expressed as functions of the quantities of direct labour and thus, in turn, as functions of 'values'.[2]

---

[1] See P. Garegnani, *Il capitale nelle teorie della distribuzione*, Milan, 1960, p. 58n.

[2] See, for example, M. Nuti, 'The Transformation of Values into Production Prices and the Marxian Theory of Exploitation', duplicated text, Cambridge, 1972. The symbols used are the same as those of section i of the appendix to the preceding

The aggregate equalities often appear in works on the transformation problem. As we saw in the previous chapter, what is involved here is either the choice of particular units of measurement for prices, or equalities between prices and values expressed in gold, obtained by means of special hypotheses. Seton speaks of them as 'postulates of invariance'.[3] The term postulates seems quite inappropriate in these cases. To *posit*, for example, that the sum of prices is equal to the sum of values (as an additional equation completely determining prices) is not to state a postulate or even an important proposition of economic theory, any more than the choice of a particular unit of measurement for weight is a postulate or important proposition in physics.[4] But we have already discussed at length why Marx's problem has nothing to do with the unit of measure adopted, nor with any particular hypotheses about the structure of production methods.

In the last analysis, however they have been conceived and presented by the authors who have worked on the problem, these transformations consist in a *determination* of prices of production and the (logically) subsequent establishment of relationships

---

chapter. The necessary quantities of directly necessary labour are linked to 'values' by the relation:

$$m = (I - A)\mu$$

Prices of production, apart from the choice of a unit of measure, are obtained from the system:

$$p = [I - A(1 + r)]^{-1} mw(1 + r)$$
$$w = fp$$

Substituting the right-hand side of the first equation into the second, we have:

$$1 = f[I - A(1 + r)]^{-1} m(1 + r)$$

This equation allows determination of r; let r* be the value thus obtained.

$$p = [I - A(1 + r^*)]^{-1} mw(1 + r^*) = [I - A(1 + r^*)]^{-1} [I - A]w(1 + r^*)\mu$$

Prices are thus obtained from 'values' through a linear transformation:

$$[I - A(1 + r^*)]^{-1} [I - A] w(1 + r^*)$$

[3] F. Seton, 'The Transformation Problem' in *The Review of Economic Studies*, 1956-1957, pp. 149-160.
[4] This analogy would collapse if the problem were to examine the changes in prices and the rate of profit consequent to variations in wages. Then the choice of a unit of measurement does have certain consequences, although it has nothing of a postulate about it (see section 2 below).

between prices of production and values, or better, quantities of embodied labour.[5]

As for Marx's idea that the analysis of prices can confirm that labour is the source of value, such arguments – to the extent that they are based on a correct determination of prices of production, or to the extent that they represent steps, however imperfect, towards such a determination – speak negatively. To the extent that such arguments are presented as solutions to the problem of the 'derivation' of prices from values, and to the extent that this problem as such is attributed to Marx, they confuse aspects of Marx's transformation that are admittedly closely linked but can and must be distinguished. Let us examine this latter point.

The proposition that prices of production result from a redistribution of surplus-value can be understood in two ways. First, however prices are obtained, it could mean that aggregate quantities of value and surplus-value are conserved, which is to say that the rate of profit is $\dfrac{S}{C + V}$; second, it could mean that prices can be obtained *only* from values through a procedure consisting of the redistribution of surplus-value as profits.

There is no doubt that Marx had in mind this second, 'stronger' meaning, namely that the determination of prices could only be a derivation from values; but it is the first that is really significant if the validity of the law of value is to be confirmed.

In other words, since Marx considered prices of production the result of the redistribution of surplus-value, his determination of them was indeed a derivation from values. More important than the general contention that prices of production can be derived from values, however, is the particular way they are derived, since if the

[5] The meaning of the following assertion, attributed to me by Roncaglia, is that the determination of prices is logically independent of the determination of values: 'It is always possible to transform 3 into 7 by multiplying it by 7/3; but what significance does it have?' (Roncaglia, *Sraffa e la teorie dei prezzi*, Bari, 1975, p. 161n). Here 7 stands for the *operation* of determining prices and 3 for the *operation* of determining values. The relationship between values and prices is established *after* the operation that determines prices, while values are left aside. If, on the other hand, 7 and 3 represent prices and values, then the remark is misplaced, for there is a 'universal' relationship between prices and values (see note 3) and not just the insignificant 7/3, which corresponds to the price of any commodity that can be ascertained from the labour embodied in it by multiplying the latter by the relation between price and embodied labour.

derivation is the one Marx held to be valid, then not only are prices determined, but the law of value is confirmed. For Marx, there is no problem of the derivation of prices from values as such; the objective is rather to determine prices and examine their divergence from values. Once it has been established that the determination Marx holds to be the only possible one, wherein the divergences between values and prices are compensated in the sum of all prices, is neither necessary nor correct, the derivation from values becomes a mere inessential aspect of the determination of prices. To continue to hold that it is the central aspect of this determination helps to confuse questions that, in the light of what is now well established about prices of production, should be sharply separated.[6]

We may conclude as follows: prices of production can indeed be derived from quantities of embodied labour, but only to the extent that these quantities, as physical measures, are substituted for natural measures, or through use of the relationship between these quantities and quantities of labour directly employed. Quantities of embodied labour are in no case transformations of *values* into prices. Marx held that embodied labour was the magnitude of value because it represented the real cost of the products. This identification raises both the problem of its confirmation in the analysis of actual exchange-values, whose relationship to quantities of embodied labour cannot be arbitrary, and the idea that such confirmation can be achieved because actual exchange-rates are determined solely by the redistribution of surplus-value, for that is the heart of the notion that labour is substance.

If we leave aside whatever claims the various 'transformations' make as regards Marx's problem, it is nonetheless the case that they

[6] Napoleoni's criticism of 'solutions' to the transformation problem emphasizes that values are unnecessary to the determination of prices (which was definitively demonstrated by Sraffa). Napoleoni has in mind the 'strong' meaning of redistribution. But the conservation of aggregate quantities alone would confirm that labour is value, however prices were obtained. Napoleoni deserves the considerable merit of having spoken to the question of the significance for Marx's problem of the mathematical systems being put forward at a time when Sraffa's system was blithely accepted as the solution to Marx's problem, with quantities of embodied labour replacing physical quantities to boot. (See, for example, Maruice Dobb's introduction to the Italian edition of *Capital* Volume 1, Rome, 1964, pp. 10-15.) Napoleoni's main works are: 'Sul problema marxiano della trasformazione', in *La Rivista Trimestrale*, 1966, nos. 17-18; *Smith, Ricardo, Marx*, Turin, 1970; *Lezioni sul capitolo VI inedito di Marx*, Turin, 1974.

have indeed definitively clarified the determination and investigation of the variations of prices of production and the rate of profit. (We are referring here to the work that preceded that of Sraffa and Garegnani, not to subsequent efforts, which have served almost exclusively to spread confusion).

At this point we must return to the distinction, mentioned at the beginning of chapter 3, between the problem of the refutation of the notion that advances of capital generate profits (expounded in the opening pages of *Capital* Volume 3) and the place of this problem in Marx's more general approach to value. As will be seen, if the question of capital as the source of profit is dealt with otherwise than it is by Marx, then the simple determination of prices of production – discarding any attempt to derive them from values – is sufficient to resolve this question while ruling out any possibility of advances of capital being regarded as an autonomous source of value. Before broaching this argument and drawing some general conclusions, however, we must pause to examine two works by Sraffa: his introduction to Ricardo's *Principles* and *Production of Commodities by Means of Commodities*.

2. Ricardo, Sraffa and Real Cost

As we have already noted, Sraffa holds that the problem of value in Ricardo's work is strictly subordinate to the determination of the rate of profit. His hypothesis that product and advances of capital were homogeneous in agriculture enabled Ricardo in his writings before the *Principles* to separate the determination and study of the variations of the rate of profit from the determination of exchange-values. The rate of profit, he argued, is determined by a ratio between quantities of wheat; the exchange-values of commodities other than wheat adjust themselves such that the rate of profit is the same for all investments.[7]

Once the 'wheat-wheat' hypothesis was abandoned – in the *Principles* and in his later work – however, Ricardo encountered a fresh problem: the magnitudes whose ratio determines the rate of

[7] Sraffa, 'Introduction' to Ricardo, *On the Principles of Political Economy and Taxation,* in *Works and Correspondence*, Cambridge, 1951, pp. xxx-xxxii.

profit depend on prices (i.e. the sum of the prices of the commodities that make up total output minus the sum of the prices of the commodities that make up advances, together with this latter amount); but prices are not known unless the rate of profit is known.

Once he has thus pin-pointed Ricardo's problem in determining the rate of profit, Sraffa then defines 'the problem of value which interested Ricardo'. It was 'how to find a measure of value which would be invariant to changes in the division of the product; for, if a rise or fall of wages by itself brought about a change in the magnitude of the social product, it would be hard to determine accurately the effect on profits'.[8] Further on, Sraffa speaks of 'the function of the theory of value' in Ricardo's work: Ricardo's aim was to make 'it possible, in the face of changes in distribution, to measure changes in the magnitude of aggregates of commodities of different kinds or, what is even more important, to ascertain its constancy'.[9] When it comes to determining the rate of profit, the heterogeneous aggregates are advances and total output. Ricardo sought a commodity such that these aggregates, when measured in it, would become independent of the rate of profit; the latter could then be determined once the aggregates were known as physical entities.

But the simultaneous constancy of two heterogeneous aggregates despite changes in the rate of profit implies the constancy of each exchange-value.[10] Yet the factors that cause exchange-values to vary with the rate of profit are the very ones that provoke differences between exchange-values and ratios of quantities of embodied labour. Hence the characteristic of the invariable measure: since it must 'neutralize' the causes of such variations, it also eliminates the differences. The absolute values of commodities (that is, exchange-values with respect to the invariable measure) must therefore be proportional to quantities of embodied labour. In other words, the only way to eliminate the variations was to eliminate the differences; but it was the variations and not the differences with which Ricardo

---

[8] Ibid., p. xlvii.

[9] Ibid., p. xlix.

[10] It is perhaps useful to recall that Ricardo's problem is insoluble if two cases are excluded: if the two aggregates are homogeneous (in which case the problem itself disappears), and if prices do not vary whatever measure is chosen (i.e. if the organic composition and turnover times of capital are equal for all investments).

was really concerned: 'Ricardo was not interested for its own sake in the problem of why two commodities produced by the same quantities of labour are not of the same exchangeable value. He was concerned with it only in so far as thereby relative values are affected by changes in wages. The two points of view of difference and of change are closely linked together; yet the search for an invariable measure of value, which is so much at the centre of Ricardo's system, arises exclusively from the second and would have no counterpart in an investigation of the first.'[11]

Sraffa's exposition of the order in which Ricardo dealt with these problems isolates and highlights the *function* of the theory of value with respect to the objective of determining – and studying variations in – the rate of profit. Ricardo sees the identity of value and labour exclusively in the context of the problem of measurement, which arose once he abandoned the hypothesis of his early works. Indeed, Ricardo subsequently disregarded this identity, implicitly treating it as a residual factor of little interest.

The case we wish to argue here is based on those passages enumerated in the introduction, in which Ricardo identifies value with embodied labour for reasons extraneous to the exchange of commodities, for example the passage from *Absolute Value and Exchangeable Value* quoted earlier. This passage is preceded by a discussion of the invariable measure as a means by which to examine variations in exchange-values over time. Ricardo interrupts his analysis of one example to reassert vehemently that value is identical to labour because of the principle of real cost. ('Every thing is originally purchased by labour – nothing that has value can be produced without it.') Shortly afterwards, labour is again posited as the basis of value *because it is labour that produces*: 'That the greater or less quantity of labour worked up in commodities can be the only cause of their alteration in value is completely made out as soon as we are agreed that all commodities are the produce of labour and would have no value but for the labour expended upon them.' He then immediately returns to the problem of the invariable measure, referring to the difficulties that arise when variations in distribution are taken into account: 'Though this is true it is still exceedingly difficult to discover or even to imagine any commodity which shall

[11] Sraffa, Introduction to *Principles*, p. xlix.

be a perfect general measure of value, as we shall see by observations which follow.'[12]

Ricardo is dealing with variations in exchange-values that result from changes in production methods and shifts in the distribution of income between wages and profits. His attempt to render this second cause inoperative leads him to the conclusion that absolute values must be proportional to quantities of embodied labour. However, this idea that it is necessary and possible to find a measure that makes exchange-values impervious to variations in wages, in other words, proportional to quantities of embodied labour (the variations can be excluded only by excluding the differences), a measure inherent in the logic of exchange, is founded on an argument that is not derived from the nature of exchange – namely that labour is the ultimate means by which objects are produced and that *consequently* value is a measure of labour expended. This is clear in the passages quoted above, in which the idea of an invariable measure is immediately connected to value and its foundation on labour on the basis of the principle of real cost: a perfect measure should exclude changes arising from variations in distribution and should thus reflect only modifications in quantities of embodied labour. This counterposition between real and apparent modifications inherent in the logic of exchange is paralleled by one external to that logic and based on a general conception of production and the role of labour within it. It is to this second counterposition that Ricardo is referring in the passages we are examining here: the perfect measure should reflect only changes in value – embodied labour – since 'all commodities are the product of labour and would have no value if labour had not been expended in their production'. (Here it should be noted that in the passage quoted in the introduction Ricardo defines value as embodied labour, *explicitly* ignoring exchange).

This concept of something independent of exchange called 'the real cost' of products and the connection of this concept with the characteristics of an invariable measure that on the contrary depends on exchange may perhaps account for the persistence in Ricardo's investigation of an idea he himself considered almost obviously untenable. To anyone examining the problems of prices of

[12] Ricardo, *Absolute Value and Exchangeable Value*, in *Works and Correspondence*, Volume IV, p. 397.

production and the rate of profit in the light of recent solutions, Ricardo's concept, extraneous as it is to the nature of exchange, may seem an obstacle to research. But at a time when there was no adequate way to broach directly the questions raised by the interdependence of prices and the rate of profit, it was the basis for the formulation of a correct and fruitful view of the mechanism of profit formation. We will return to this at greater length below.

There are thus two interwoven aspects of Ricardo's discussion of the invariable measure: its function in the context of the theory of profit, and the principle of real cost, which Ricardo emphatically reasserts from time to time, almost as if to counterpose a higher 'rationality' and 'reality' to variations in exchange-values that do not result from changes in production methods. Of these two aspects, Sraffa emphasizes only the first, neglecting the second. Indeed, one of the major points of *Production of Commodities by Means of Commodities* is that the rate of profit can and must be determined without recourse to any concept extraneous to the logic of exchange. Given wages in terms of any commodity, the quantities of labour directly required and the quantities of commodities produced and employed in each industry (in other words, the methods of production) are all that is necessary to determine both the rate of profit and prices of production. The methods of production, which are descriptions of industries, can be replaced by 'quantities of dated labour'.[13] The description of industries through successive quantities of dated labour is fully equivalent to the description through methods of production (except if the wage is zero). It should be noted that it is essential to know the *distribution* in 'time' of the labour expended in the production of commodities. Both for methods of production and for successive quantities of dated labour, we are dealing with aggregate magnitudes computed from material production solely in order to determine prices and the rate of profit.[14]

---

[13] In other words, each industry can be described in terms of a sequence of quantities of labour, in which the first term is directly necessary labour, the second the labour directly necessary for the production of the means of production employed, the third the quantities of labour directly necessary to produce the means of production which, in turn, enter into the production of means of production directly employed, and so on. The sum of these quantities of labour is the labour embodied in the product of the industry in question.

[14] The analytical difficulty common to classical theory, Marx's theory, and the

This reduction of methods of production to quantities of dated labour makes it possible to show very simply that the rate of profit may be determined once wages are given in terms of any commodity, and to study how the rate of profit varies with wages. If wages are given in terms of commodity a[15] and if this commodity is also chosen as the measure of prices and wages, we have:

$$Ap_a = L_a w + L_{al}(1 + r) + \ldots$$

where L_a, L_{al}, ... are the quantities of labour required at different times to produce the quantity A of the commodity a. It is immediately apparent that the rate of profit is determined once wages are given and that as wages rise the rate of profit falls (the coefficients of the series are quantities of labour and are therefore positive).

Sraffa's 'invariable measure' – the standard commodity – is less significant and sometimes overestimated,[16] although not by Sraffa. This measure guarantees the invariability neither of prices of production nor of the aggregates discussed above as wages vary; it corresponds to Ricardo's invariable measure only to the extent that it is similar to the 'wheat' of those of his works that precede the *Principles*. The value of the totality of its means of production as expressed in this measure does not vary with distribution.

In other words, Sraffa shows that within the real system, with given inputs and outputs, there is hidden an 'industry' that can be obtained by bringing together proper portions of real industries such that the 'commodity' (generally composite) produced by this industry is identical in composition to the aggregate of its means of production. If wages are expressed in terms of that commodity, then the rate of profit of the real system can be immediately determined as a ratio of two quantities of that commodity, without any need to determine prices. Furthermore, if wages as expressed in the standard

marginal theory of distribution has been formulated in these terms by Garegnani, *Il capitale nelle teorie della distribuzione*, Milan, 1960: 'What is required is to "measure" capital in terms that are independent of variations in distribution and that, at the same time, are identifiably related to the value of capital' (p. vii). Garegnani argues that whereas marginal theory requires a measure for capital in terms of a single magnitude, the difficulties of classical theory can be overcome by 'measuring' capital in terms of a set of quantities (ibid., p. viii).

[15] Here, in contrast to the previous chapter, we are using Sraffa's notation. We shall also assume, as Sraffa did in *Production of Commodities by Means of Commodities*, that wages are paid at the end of the period of production.

[16] Examples of this will be examined in section 6 below.

commodity vary, the rate of profit varies inversely, as follows directly from the way it is determined (and again, there is no need to study variations in prices).

There is, however, one important difference between the standard commodity and the 'wheat' of Ricardo's early work. There, wages were directly *expressed* in terms of wheat because they were *given* in terms of wheat (indeed, they could be *paid* in a money-commodity; in that case, the amount would be determined along with the prices of commodities other than wheat after determination of the rate of profit). But when that particular hypothesis about agriculture and wages is abandoned, the relationship between the rate of profit and the wage rate as expressed in the standard commodity appears to have a purely interpretative function. This point is exemplified by the fact that when this relationship is used to prove propositions in which wages are expressed in some other commodity, it must always be accompanied by other arguments designed to support the proposition without reference to the standard commodity. To clarify this point, let us examine the argumentation by which Sraffa arrives at the following assertion: 'if the wage is cut in terms of *any* commodity ... the rate of profits will rise; and vice versa for an increase of the wage.'[17] Sraffa proceeds thus: first he considers the reduction equation for a commodity:

$$Ap_1 = L_a w + L_{a1} w(1 + r) + \ldots$$

where p_a and w are expressed in the standard commodity. He then uses the linear relationship between w and r (which he has established previously) to conclude that when w falls and r rises, $\frac{p_a}{w}$ rises. Next, he notes that $\frac{p_a}{w}$ does not depend on the measure used for p_a and w. Thus, if r rises, regardless of how prices and wages are measured, then prices rise relative to wages, which is the proposition to be demonstrated.

As we have seen, however, the same conclusion can be reached directly by simply measuring prices and wages in terms of the commodity with respect to which wages, the independent variable, fall.[18]

---

[17] *Production of Commodities by Means of Commodities*, p. 40.

[18] Sraffa also employs another argument to prove that a price cannot fall in greater proportion than the wage when both are expressed in the standard commodity. Let us

In sum, then, the standard commodity is a purely subjective device that may be useful in rendering the subject matter in question more easily comprehensible; it is not at all indispensable to the substantiation of the major propositions of the theory. (In this respect it is similar to the discussion of variations of relative prices in terms of 'surplus' and 'deficit' industries created by changes in wages unaccompanied by changes in prices).

The preceding paragraphs have been directed primarily against overestimation of the standard commodity, which has a purely heuristic function in Sraffa's book and does not figure amongst its 'central propositions'.[19] We have dwelt on Sraffa's work in order to

suppose that some prices do fall in greater proportion than wages and then consider the price of the product 'whose rate of fall exceeds that of all the others', call it p_a. From the equation (in which prices and wages are all expressed in the standard commodity):

$$Ap_a = (A_a p_a + B_a p_b + \ldots + K_a p_k)(1 + r) + L_a w$$

it is immediately evident that since the rate of profit rises when w falls (as shown by the relation found for wages expressed in the standard commodity), p_a can fall in greater proportion than the wage only if the totality of the means of production of commodity a falls in greater proportion than does p_a; but that contradicts our assumption about p_a (*Production of Commodities by Means of Commodities*, p. 40). The idea on which this argument is based – recourse to the commodity that contradicts the thesis most strongly (which is mathematically possible because the number of commodities is finite) – can also be used, without any reference to the standard commodity, to demonstrate that variations in wages expressed in any commodity vary inversely with the rate of profit. Let us suppose that the rate of profit rises. We must prove that all prices measured in labour rise (i.e. that wages expressed in any commodity fall). Let us posit the (absurd) proposition that some prices fall, and let p_a be the one that falls in the greatest proportion. Let us now examine its equation (in which all prices and wages are measured in labour commanded):

$$Ap_a = (A_a p_a + B_a p_a + \ldots + K_a p_k)(1 + r) + L_a$$

Since we have assumed that r rises while p_a falls, the totality of its means of production must fall even more than p_a itself. But that contradicts the assumed property of p_a. Finally, if we use the procedure of reduction to quantities of dated labour to show that the rate of profit and wages expressed in terms of any particular commodity vary inversely, then it is convenient to use that same commodity as a measure; if we employ the reasoning presented in this note, it is better to measure in terms of labour commanded (in fact, even under the reduction, it is immediately apparent that a rise in the rate of profit entails a rise in all prices in labour commanded, i.e. the fall in wages in terms of any commodity).

[19] Ibid., p. iv; in this connection see also Roncaglia, *Sraffa e la teoria dei prezzi*, Bari, 1975, chapter 3. It should be noted, however, that while Sraffa defines the standard commodity as a 'purely auxiliary construction' (p. 31) for establishing the proportional relation between variations in the rate of profit and in wages (where, in fact, its elimination requires either the *positing* of the proportional relation as an addi-

establish the ideas and conclusions that make it possible to preserve the deeper meaning of many of Marx's own assertions. The following section shall be devoted to the exposition of a line of interpretation that seeks to do for Marx what Sraffa did for Ricardo – to isolate and analyse the function of value in his theory.

3. Profit and Surplus Labour

Let us now return to Marx's critique of the idea that capital is the source of profit and the role of the labour theory of value in this critique. As we have seen, the origins of this idea lie in Smith's contention that exchange occurred in proportion to embodied labour only in the period prior to capitalism and that profit is an autonomous component of price determined independently of wages.[20]

Ricardo's attempt to demonstrate that Smith's position was incorrect was never carried to completion, for difficulties were encountered in considering the uniformity of the rate of profit. The gaps in Ricardo's analysis, Marx argued, had enabled Smith's interpretation to survive: 'Malthus bases his polemic against Ricardo's definition of value entirely on the principles advanced by Ricardo himself, to the effect that variations in the exchangeable values of commodities, independent of the labour worked up in them, are produced by the different composition of capital as resulting from the process of circulation. ... In short, on Ricardo's confusing cost-price with value and regarding the equalisation of cost-prices, which are independent of the mass of labour employed in the particular spheres of production, as modifications of value itself, thereby throwing the whole principle overboard. Malthus seizes on these contradictions in the determination of value by labour-time – contradictions that were first discovered and emphasised by Ricardo himself – not in order to solve them but in order to relapse into quite meaningless conceptions and to pass off the mere *formulation* of contradictory phenomena, their expression in speech, as their

tional equation, without knowing what measure is implied, or measurement in terms of a quantity of labour that varies with the rate of profit), he subsequently employs the linear relation, with the sole effect of complicating the proof, in studying the shift in the rate of profit with variations in wages expressed in terms of any commodity.

[20] I leave aside rent, which Smith held to be another component of price.

solution.'[21] And further: 'Malthus uses the material provided by Ricardo against the law of value, and turns it against him.'[22]

Smith begins with the mere existence of profit and concludes that it is an autonomous source of value; Malthus begins with the unresolved difficulties of Ricardo's treatment of exchange-values – namely Ricardo's uncertainties about the uniformity of the rate of profit – and again concludes that profit is an autonomously determined addition. More particularly, Malthus's idea that the profit contained in the price of a commodity is a 'surplus above the labour embodied in the commodity'[23] is directly derived from Smith's original confusion between the value of labour-power and the value that labour-power adds to the means of production. Profit is therefore to be accounted for by exchange, while surplus-value is said to result because 'the seller sells the commodity *above* its value (i.e., for more labour-time than is contained in it)'.[24] However, 'What he thus gains as a seller of a commodity, he loses as a buyer of another and it is absolutely impossible to discover what profit is to be made in reality from such a general nominal price increase. It is in particular difficult to understand how society as a whole can enrich itself in this way, how a real surplus-value or surplus product can thus arise.'[25]

The passages devoted to Malthus (and to Torrens) in the third volume of *Theories of Surplus-Value* deal with the same themes as chapter 4 of *Capital* Volume 1 and the opening chapters of *Capital* Volume 3, where Marx broaches the problem of the origin of profit. His argumentation is composed of two different strands, which are woven together by Marx but can in fact be disentangled.

Let us begin with the first strand. The idea that profit is an addition to the labour embodied in commodities, Marx argues, obscures the 'material' basis of profit, which is surplus labour. In other words, if there are profits, they represent purchasing power over a portion of total social product. In that case, however, the total labour-time expended is necessarily greater than that embodied in

[21] Marx, *Theories of Surplus Value*, Volume III, London, 1969, p. 29. Here 'cost-price' is the translation of 'Kostpreis'; here too (see note 13, p. 43), we must understand 'price of production'.

[22] Ibid., p. 29

[23] Ibid., p. 26.

[24] Ibid., p. 20.

[25] Ibid., p. 20.

the commodities acquired by the workers. This aspect of Marx's argument emerges with particular clarity in another passage directed against Malthus. Marx begins by assuming that the value of money given in exchange for labour-power is equal to the value the worker adds to the means of production. In that case, 'profit can only arise from a surcharge added by the seller over and above the *real* value of the commodity'.[26] Then he considers the capitalists in the wage-goods sector. They can make a profit as follows: 'The commodities for which they paid the workers 100 thaler will be sold back again to them for 110 thaler. That means that they will only sell 10/11 of the product back to the workers and retain 1/11 for themselves. But what else does that mean but that the worker who, for example, works for 11 hours, gets paid for only 10 hours; that he is given the product of only 10 hours, while the capitalist receives one hour or the product of one hour without giving any equivalent.'[27]

This passage is particularly significant, because in it Marx goes so far as to admit the possibility that real wages may be determined not directly by the relationship between labour-power and capital, but indirectly by the capitalists' ability to make additions to the cost-price. But he does so only to conclude that profits, however determined, cannot exist without surplus labour.[28]

Marx replies to the idea that profits originate from exchange by asking this question: 'Where do the funds for the profit come from, where does the surplus product in which the surplus-value manifests itself come from?'[29] The answer, it bears repeating, is based on a precise distinction between the labour that labour-power adds to the means of production and the labour embodied in the commodities for which wages are exchanged.

This analysis in terms of embodied labour, which Marx counter-poses to irrational views based on the superficial observation of prices, is connected to his determination of prices of production and the rate of profit. This brings us to the second aspect of his argumentation. If one begins with commodities and the profits

[26] Ibid., p. 32.
[27] Ibid., p. 33.
[28] Implicitly, Marx is admitting here that the money-commodity is not exchanged for other commodities according to the norm governing the exchange of these commodities amongst themselves. We shall return to this point in the next section.
[29] *Theories of Surplus-Value*, Volume 3, p. 32.

contained in them, one must conclude that surplus labour is a precondition of profits. Moreover, surplus labour furnishes an exact measure of the amount of profits. But the idea that profit is an autonomous source of value can also be criticized from the standpoint of exchange. Indeed, profits are determined the moment wages are given in terms of commodities, and it thereby becomes impossible to consider these profits an independent addition to the labour embodied in commodities. Marx's transformation (by which we mean, here as elsewhere, the result he considered correct) leads to the contention that profits *are* surplus labour and are *therefore* constituted by the difference between the labour embodied in wages and the total labour expended. Once again, then, if wages are given in terms of commodities, then the fraction of total labour expended required to reconstitute them is also given, while the remaining fraction produces the 'surplus product in which the surplus-value manifests itself'. The magnitude of this surplus-value is precisely the magnitude of total profit.

The analysis of production in terms of embodied labour, the specification of the value added by labour-power, and finally, the subsequent transformation enable Marx to uncover the surplus labour concealed behind profits and *simultaneously* to depict prices of production precisely. He thereby clarifies the points Ricardo had left unsolved, which had made possible the persistence of Smith's error.

Now, keeping in mind the correct solution to the problem of prices of production, let us re-examine these two aspects of Marx's criticism. We shall find that their unity on the basis of the labour theory of value must be sundered (which overturns the theory that profit is redistributed surplus-value); but each of the two aspects, taken singly, can be fully maintained. First, the assertion that so long as there are profits, however determined (and even apart from uniformity of profit distribution), there must be surplus-value is completely independent of the theory of value and prices. It arises strictly from the analysis based on embodied labour and from the simple observation that profits represent purchasing power over portions of total output.[30] Second, if the contention that capital advances are the source of profit is directly assaulted on the field of

---

[30] For further elaboration and clarification of this actually quite simple point, see the appendix to this chapter.

prices of production, Sraffa's analysis can resolve all the difficulties. The possibility that there may be some source of value other than labour is ruled out by extirpating the problem of the 'source' of value itself. The analysis of prices of production disposes of the idea that labour is the 'wellspring' of value, while the valid concept this idea had generated − that profits are subtractions from wages − is maintained.

The conclusions presented by Sraffa and Garegnani in the early sixties, and the approach based on separating the labour theory of value from labour-value as such (described above in the discussion of Sraffa's introduction to Ricardo's *Principles*) have given rise to various attempts to re-interpret and reformulate Marx's theory. The most noteworthy of these was presented by F. Vianello in 1970.[31] He emphasized the results obtained by 'analysis of value', by which he meant the first point stated above, that the surplus product that underpins profits is real, as is the surplus labour corresponding to it. In particular, basing himself on the vertical integration of industries, Vianello showed that the total employed work force may be viewed as divided into two parts, one which produces, directly and indirectly, the aggregate of wage-goods, and another which produces directly and indirectly, the surplus product. In this manner, Vianello argues, it is possible 'to see' a characteristic of the work force as a whole that is hidden from each individual worker by the division of labour, a characteristic that is immediately evident under some pre-capitalist forms of exploitation, the corvée for example. It is this: the toiler labours for himself during part of the working day, while the remainder is estranged from him in favour of those who take no part in production.[32]

In this context, Vianello views the analysis of value as a useful cognitive instrument (he maintains that Marx's analysis of value is 'primarily an *analysis of the division of labour* in a society based on exchange'[33]); but when it comes to prices of production, he is well aware that the various 'transformations' are useless and he therefore determines these prices directly from the methods of production,

---

[31] F. Vianello, *Valore, prezzi e distribuzione del reddito*, Rome, 1970.

[32] In his 'Plusvalore e profitto nell'analisi di Marx', in Sylos Labini (ed.), *Prezzi relativi e distribuzione del reddito*, Turin, 1973, Vianello ascribes to Marx a 'vision' of vertically integrated sectors.

[33] Ibid., p. 89.

without relating them to values.[34] It is my view that Vianello does not make it clear that what he is really talking about is the role the concept of embodied labour can play: but he is not talking about embodied labour *as value* in the sense that Marx does. Thus, while his rejection of spurious solutions is wholly lucid, he gives the impression that he would like to defend the labour theory of value even though he implicitly discards it.

But the more important question, on which Vianello places great emphasis, is this: analysis in terms of embodied labour permits the revealing of the exploitation concealed by prices of production, namely the extraction of surplus labour. This is a characteristic capitalism shares with all the modes of production that preceded it. There is no doubt that this is just what Marx meant when he spoke of exploitation and that to some extent his concern was precisely to uncover the surplus labour that lies behind prices. There is no need to marshal a long list of quotations to support this thesis; it is sufficient to note the opening passage of section 2 of chapter 10 of *Capital* Volume 1, which begins: 'Capital did not invent surplus labour', and concludes with a list of the exploiting classes of history, capitalists included. This is a vital point and cannot be left at the mere observation that Marx considered surplus labour and hence exploitation a feature capitalism shares with other modes of production. The problem is rather to establish the relative importance of this proposition in Marx's theoretical system and to locate it in the theoretical framework we are now considering.

The authors against whom Marx argues that surplus labour is the reality that lies behind prices are, principally, Smith with his idea of prices as the addition of autonomous components, Malthus, and Torrens. These writers do, however, share one premise with Ricardo and Marx: when discussing value, they reason on the basis of a *given* total production. Marx therefore counterposes surplus labour to their positions on profit, which are wholly irrational in the light of this common premise.[35] But the existence of surplus labour behind

[34] Vianello's book, however, does include an attempt to establish a relation between the rate of surplus-value and the rate of profit, which is not very significant, in my view. (See chapters 5 and 6.)

[35] Marx pays little attention to the origins of a theory of profits based on the notion of a 'contribution' by the capitalist. The authors that he considered truly important adversaries, and to whom he devoted most attention, are the same as those Ricardo had dealt with. Senior, for example, is treated with contempt, consigned to the ranks

profit cannot be used – as it often is nowadays – as an argument against the marginal theory of distribution, for here the premises are no longer those of the classical economists. Output is not a given in the theory of value: it is a variable, and the fraction of net production that becomes the capitalists' income is related to the increase in product generated by a marginal increase in capital. No self-respecting marginalist would deny that the labour embodied in wage-goods is less than the labour embodied in the net product.

Marginal theory must be assailed – and has been, successfully – on a different field of battle: it must be demonstrated that it is impossible to formulate a coherent and meaningful theory of profit based upon the marginal productivity of capital.[36]

Let us now leave marginal theory and return to Marx. We have stressed the vital role of exploitation, or the extraction of surplus labour, in the refutation of the idea that capital is the source of profit. We have likewise seen that the demonstration that surplus-value is the basis of profit constituted a definitive confutation of the absurd material analyses of production Marx was attacking. But there was more. The theory of prices of production and the assertion that they could be reduced to labour rendered that confutation a consequence of the positive affirmation that labour is the sole cost. Marx thereby negated not only *those* apologetic propositions but also every possible alternative (given Marx's horizon, itself limited

of vulgar economists. (See, for example, *Capital* Volume 1, pp. 333-338; on Senior and the reaction against Ricardo during the 1830s, see Dobb, *Theories of Value and Distribution Since Adam Smith*, Cambridge, 1973, chapter 4.)

[36] In *Production of Commodities by Means of Commodities* Sraffa undertakes to provide the 'prelude to a critique of economic theory', economic theory here being understood as the 'marginal theory' of value and distribution. On this basis, it has been demonstrated that it is impossible to establish a relation between the rate of interest and the value of total capital invested that can be interpreted as a demand function. (For a comprehensive review of this debate see G. Harcourt, *Some Cambridge Controversies in the Theory of Capital*, Cambridge, 1972.) For an effective critique of Wicksell's and Walras's theories see Garegnani, *Il capitale nelle teorie della distribuzione*. There remain some theories of general equilibrium inspired by marginalist theory (Arrow, Debreu, Hahn, Malinvaud). In their work the lack of difficulty in determining equilibrium is achieved at the price of drifting quite far from the problematic that was central to the theories of both classicists and 'classical' marginalists, from quite different points of view. For an attempt to lay the basis of a systematic critique of these theories, see Garegnani, 'On a Change in the Notion of Equilibrium in Recent Works on Value and Distribution: a Comment on Samuelson', in Brown, Sato, Zarembka (eds.), *Essays in Modern Capital Theory*, North Holland, 1976.

by the classical premises). The comparison with past modes of production was then effected on the basis of a law common to them all, obvious in pre-capitalist periods, demonstrated by science in the era of capitalism.

The assertion that capitalism exhibits a universal law under which labour stands at the centre of production burdens Marx's propositions about a continuity between the conditions of labour under capitalism and in earlier times with 'positivity'. Once it is recognized that it is impossible to rigorously posit labour as the sole real cost (in other words, to assert that general law), then the observation that the capitalist mode of production has exploitation in common with preceding modes, and similar assertions as well, acquire different meanings. They are then valid for what they *deny* – for the refutation they imply and on which they are based, of any apology for profit – rather than for what they affirm.[37]

But the most important aspect of Marx's discussion of exploitation is the second one, where he concentrates on the features that distinguish capitalist exploitation from all previously existing forms. Surplus labour is counterposed to the notion that profit arises from exchange, since surplus labour is the material precondition for the existence of profit. But the point then is to understand *how* it is possible to extract surplus labour under a system of social relations that arises from the elimination of the direct subordination of individuals (this question will be discussed more fully in the following section). Moreover, while combatting the potentially apologetic mystification upheld by Ricardo's opponents, Marx also advanced the thesis that capitalism promoted a historically unprecedented expansion of the productive forces. In this context, he viewed the capitalist primarily as 'the servant of capital', the unwitting agent of accumulation. Marx's whole analysis is not so much designed to emphasize the relationship of exploitation on which this accumulation is based; rather, his aim is to expose this relationship and to combat any apologetic attempts in order to pinpoint both the true function of capitalism in history and the real

---

[37] As we have noted, it is necessary to distinguish carefully between the apologetic ideas about profit Marx had in mind and ideas based on the marginal theory of value, for the two sets of ideas must be refuted in different ways. In the final chapter we shall discuss in more general terms the change in outlook that must accompany the retention of substantive points of Marx's theory.

roots of its necessary disappearance. We will return to the latter point – Marx's development of the idea of the anarchy of commodity production in the theory of crises – in the last chapter.

It is useful at this point to return to Vianello's interpretation of Marx. He distinguishes and isolates the various functions of the labour theory of value in Marx's argument, leaving aside all that has to do with the development of the idea that labour is real cost and the approach connected to it, emphasizing what can be preserved. Good reasons for neglect of the themes to which such great attention has been paid in this book can be found if Marx's work is read primarily through the prism of the critical tasks to which the labour theory of value is directed. It could then be maintained that the idea that embodied labour constitutes real cost is important for what it refutes rather than for what it affirms. When Marx counterposes embodied labour as real cost to cost price – i.e., capitalist cost[38] – his aim is to refute the theory that profit is an extra arising from exchange; in any event, Smith, progenitor of the idea that profit is an autonomous source of value, did indeed confuse cost price and value. In the passages of the *Grundrisse* in which Marx counterposes labour as positive activity to Smith's concept of labour as sacrifice[39] it is evident that his point of departure is the refutation of Senior's contention that the 'sacrifice' made by the capitalist should be *added* to labour as a part of cost.

Denial that capital is a source of value in any sense and determination of profits as a subtraction from wages are the elements of the 'rational kernel' of the thesis that labour is real cost. The point here, however, is not to discuss whether this can also serve as a starting point for the *reconstruction* of the development of Marx's thought. Our emphasis has been the autonomy that the thesis that labour is real social cost acquires Marx's work, its development independent of the problem of exchange, and the dominant role it plays as both approach and premise in Marx's determination of prices of production. What was Ricardo's point of departure for an investigation centred on the problem of the rate of profit becomes for Marx the basis of a *systematic* treatment of all phenomena related to the production and exchange of commodities under capitalist conditions.

[38] See the passage from *Capital* Volume 3, p. 26 cited in the previous chapter.
[39] See section 1 of chapter 2.

The necessity of fully highlighting the naturalist element that constitutes the *explicit* basis of Marx's labour theory of value becomes evident if one considers the tradition that began with Marx, especially the research of recent years on Marx's themes. The lack of any critical analysis of the notion of a law of production in general and of the contention that this law necessarily asserts itself under commodity production as the law of value (or, worse yet, outright disregard for Marx's explicit motivation for his identification of value and labour) has led to a division of Marxist ranks into two trends: a paralysing orthodoxy and unconvincing attempts to reformulate Marx's propositions.

At bottom, this is the defect of Vianello's book: he locates and develops what we have called the 'rational kernel' of the theory of value without first identifying and explicitly eliminating the naturalistic element in which Marx envelops this kernel. On the other hand, since the orthodox school regards the loss of the form Marx's analysis possesses when based on the labour theory of value as tantamount to the demolition of every proposition on which Marx's construction rests, works like Vianello's encounter almost insuperable opposition.

It should be clear by now that my own book is in no way an attempt at conciliation. On the contrary, I hold that the way forward begins with Sraffa's definitive clarification of the problems left unresolved by both Marx and the classical economists. But the acceptance of these results and their integration into the body of Marxism is impossible without profound changes and radical excisions. Most important of all, the foundation upon which Marx holds the entire construction to be based must be laid bare and subjected to criticism.

4. The Value of Labour-Power and 'Equal Exchange'

The proposition that profit originates in exchange has two different meanings as criticized by Marx. To the first Marx counterposes surplus labour as the precondition of profit. But the idea that exchange can generate profit does not necessarily entail the error in the material analysis of production Marx ascribes to Malthus. Precisely in one of the passages directed against Malthus – one of those cited above – Marx admits, though only for an instant, the possibility that profit may be obtained through price increases. An examination of this point will lead us to a discussion of the concepts of the value of labour-power and of 'equal exchange' between the latter and capital.

In chapter 20 of *Capital* Volume 3 Marx describes how capital, in the form of commercial capital, obtained profits before the rise of capitalism in the proper sense of the word. There is no need to burden the argument with lengthy quotations, for the crux of the matter is quite simple. The operation $M - C - M^1$ was based on circulation, on 'buying cheap to sell dear', and profit was therefore 'profit upon alienation'. In the final analysis, the source of this profit lay in the inability of the producers to dispense with the mediating services of the commercial capitalist, and in the feeble competition among the commercial capitalists themselves: 'So long as merchant's capital promotes the exchange of products between undeveloped societies, commercial profit not only appears as outbargaining and cheating, but also largely originates from them.'[40] Now, if one reads chapter 5 of *Capital* Volume 1 while bearing in mind this section of Volume 3, one cannot help noticing a close kinship between the two arguments. In Volume 3 we are told: 'To buy cheap in order to sell dear is the rule of trade. Hence, not the exchange of equivalents.'[41] But the problem of surplus-value under developed capitalism must be approached on the assumption that commodities are exchanged at their value: 'The transformation of money into capital has to be developed on the basis of the immanent laws of the exchange of commodities, in such a way that the starting-point is the exchange of equivalents.'[42]

The feature that distinguishes capitalism properly so called from the era of commercial capital, then, is embodied in the fact that the problem of profit must now be examined under the hypothesis of exchange according to value. This hypothesis brings together two distinct objectives. First, 'profit upon alienation' must be excluded. Marx's argumentation can be summarized thus: in exchange, any privilege of buyer or of seller is a privilege enjoyed by all

---

[40] *Capital* Volume 3, p. 330.
[41] Ibid., p. 329.
[42] *Capital* Volume 1, p. 268.

simultaneously. Second, the hypothesis of exchange of equivalents is accompanied by a distinction between value and market price. This implies not only the exclusion of profit upon alienation, but also abstraction from profits and losses caused by fluctuations in market prices. Thus: 'the formation of capital must be possible even though the price and value of a commodity be the same'.[43]

Inverting the order of these two points, we note that on the one hand 'normal' profits must be explained; on the other hand, in no sense can these normal profits be considered profits upon alienation. Marx's solution to the problem is, of course, well known. Since surplus-value cannot arise from buying cheap and selling dear (every commodity being sold at its value), it can originate only from the transformation, in production, of the commodities bought by the capitalist with money. The value of the commodities produced consists exactly in the value of the means of production plus the living labour employed. But what the capitalist has paid for is not this living labour but rather the value of the labour-power, the use-value of which is precisely the performance of living labour. Further, the value of labour-power, like the value of all commodities, is determined by the labour required to produce it, which in this case is fixed by the consumer goods necessary to sustain the worker.

We shall return to this point shortly. For the moment, however, let us see whether Marx's argumentation is linked indissolubly to the labour theory of value. Can the entire problem be formulated in another way? If the hypothesis of exchange according to value is to exclude profit upon alienation, care must be taken to ensure that both labour-power and whatever wages are paid with are included amongst the commodities assumed to exchange at their value. In other words, what is really important is not that, say, steel and wheat be exchanged according to the quantities of labour embodied in them, but rather that the money paid out in exchange for labour-power purchase commodities that contain exactly the quantity of labour represented by the value of the money and the value of the labour power. In sum, once money is exchanged for labour-power, profits are fixed once and for all and thus originate solely in this exchange. Let us now try to reformulate this line of argument. The primary function of exchange according to value is to rule out the

[43] Ibid., p. 269n.

possibility of profits originating, either temporarily or systematically, from differences in price at varying times or places. This is done equally well by the system of prices of production. The possibility of profit upon alienation of the sort described in chapter 20 of *Capital* Volume 3 is thus excluded.[44]

There is, however, another way to lend meaning to the idea of profit upon alienation. Profit could originate in the capacity of the capitalists to raise the purchase price, a capacity the possessors of labour-power lack. It is here that the second function of the hypothesis of exchange at value becomes relevant. Once the exchange ratio between labour-power and money is given, all exchange ratios both between labour-power and other commodities and among these commodities are fixed. Everything therefore depends on the exchange of money for labour-power. In this respect too, prices of production can be substituted for values.

The hypothesis of exchange at value, however, has an even stronger implication if its function is formulated in this manner; not only that the exchange ratios of commodities are determined once the exchange ratio between labour-power and money is determined, but also that they are independent of that ratio. This, however, is actually inessential, since what needs to be established is only that once the exchange between labour-power and capital has occurred, there is no other way to extract profit, for everything has already been decided.

To put it another way, what makes the exchange between labour and capital 'equal' is not that labour-power is exchanged for the money wage exactly in accordance with embodied labour, but that this exchange definitively determines how much of any commodity labour-power can purchase. Buyer and seller meet and freely conclude an exchange the content of which will not be subsequently modified by any ability of the capitalists to raise prices relative to the commodity in which labour-power has been paid.

Let us approach the question from yet another angle. According to the hypothesis of exchange at value, the exchange of money for labour-power is a special case of the exchange of any two commodi-

[44] To base both prices of production and exchange-values on values is to presuppose a single market in which the units of every commodity have the same price in every exchange. This is a historically significant abstraction precisely with respect to the transition from the dominance of commercial capital to that of industrial capital.

ties: the norm of embodied labour is valid universally. If the argument is put directly in terms of prices of production, however, a pronounced asymmetry appears to arise, since as long as the exchange ratio between labour-power and money is not determined, neither are the exchange ratios of other commodities. But here again the difference is only apparent. Carefully considered, the essential element of Marx's definition of the value ôf labour-power lies not in that it is a certain quantity of embodied labour, but rather in the way this quantity is defined. The generalization of commodity production and the simultaneous complete separation of the workers from the means of production turn labour-power itself into a commodity. In itself this implies a separation between what is given in exchange for this commodity and the use to which it can be put once it has been purchased. The transformation of labour-power into a commodity itself entails an objective social process through which it acquires a reproduction cost just like any other commodity. The *socially objective* character of the cost of the reproduction of labour-power means that in general certain quantities of given commodities must be considered 'normal' subsistence, even by the workers themselves. Hence the standard of normal habits of consumption in the definition of the normal wage.[45]

It is therefore clear that the labour theory of value is relevant to the definition both of labour-power as a commodity and of equal exchange only because of the role it plays. The essential elements of Marx's argument are: first, the definition of the historical conditions under which labour-power becomes a commodity and the consequent establishment of the subsistence wage as an objective social category; second, the determination of distribution in the direct exchange between capital and labour-power – the equality of this exchange means that the capitalists and workers, as free and equal owners of commodities, cannot alter what they have received from this exchange.

Profits and the appearance (socially, the reality) that the exchange between labour-power and capital is equal result from the *independence* of wages with respect to the way labour-power is used and

---

[45] We shall not dwell on Marx's elaboration of the mechanisms that drive wages back towards their normal level when they diverge from it; this involves the interrelationships among accumulation, changes in production methods, and the size of the reserve army of labour, all of which are discussed in *Capital* Volume 1, chapter 23.

from the acceptance of a given wage as *equivalent* to the labour-power yielded, since it covers its cost of production. This has a meaning different from the theory that profits 'originate' from surplus labour. It is no longer a matter of analysing production in terms of embodied labour, from which it follows that surplus labour is the material precondition for profit. Rather, the origin of profits lies in a social relationship: the reduction of labour-power to a commodity and the manner in which its price is socially determined make it *possible* for surplus labour to appear in commodity production.[46]

All this can be conserved, for it is not linked indissolubly to the labour theory of value. What should rather be carefully discussed is whether it is possible to uphold a theory of wages based on the notion of subsistence, even if historically determined, under present-day capitalism. In particular, it does not seem that wage bargaining in money terms and the complexities of inflation, with the central role played by monetary authorities, can be considered specific instances of the theory of wages of Marx and the classical economists.

5. The Response to Sraffa: Two Orthodoxies

If prices cannot be obtained from values in the manner Marx indicated, then all his propositions concerning the nature of capitalist production, formulated as they are in the terms and language of the labour theory of value, must be profoundly and carefully reconsidered. Such has not been the attitude of 'orthodox' Marxists, however. The approach common among them is exemplified by the

[46] It is only in this second sense that Marx speaks of 'swindles' and 'cheating' as sources of commercial profit in the era of commercial capital. Under developed capitalism, on the other hand, he sees commercial profit as the transfer to the commercial capitalists of a surplus-value already obtained by industrial capitalists. The difference between the two meanings of the 'origin' of profit as Marx sees it is clear from the passage against Malthus discussed in the preceding section. Marx ignores the question of whether or not profit arises from the ability of the capitalists to add to the cost-price; in other words, he leaves aside the social relations from which profit arises, but nevertheless asserts that its origin lies in surplus labour. On the centrality of this aspect of Marx's concept of labour-power, i.e. the characteristics assumed by exploitation under capitalism, see Dobb's introduction to the Italian translation of *Capital* Volume 1 (Rome, 1964) and B. Rowthorn, 'Neo-Classicism, Neo-Ricardianism, and Marxism', in *New Left Review*, no. 86, 1974.

violent attack on Sraffa and the 'neo-Ricardians' by M. Lebowitz in his article 'Current Crisis of Economic Theory'.[47] This article, which offers an outstanding example of polemic through the counterposition of quotations to arguments, accuses Sraffa of a variety of sins: 'treatment of capital as a thing rather than as a relation, the inability to explain clearly the source of profits, the tendency to find formal solutions which began from surface forms as a premise, the conception of production relations as natural rather than historical.'[48]

Sraffa was concerned to determine prices under the assumption that the rate of profit was uniform. In reality, as he has shown and contrary to what Marx thought, this is a problem of economic theory in its own right. In so doing, Sraffa demonstrated that some of the quantitative relationships among the 'surface forms' can be investigated without recourse to 'deeper explanations'. In other words, he confined himself to analysing magnitudes that Marx thought could be obtained only by starting from values; but the reason for this deliberate limitation has nothing to do with any alleged 'vulgarity' of the author's approach, as is often blithely assumed. On the contrary, the limitation is integral to the analysis. The difference from Marx is profound, and it is useful to emphasize it, but it is vital to understand that the problems Sraffa's analysis implies for Marxist economists are crucial. They must be faced squarely, and not avoided through empty chatter about grand themes — such as that capital is a social relationship or that the social relations of production are historically determined — reducing to mere rhetoric terms that Marx defined with great precision. For Marx these themes were not incantations to be invoked as a prelude to scientific analysis, but were fused with it and determined its development; while at the same time proof and refinement of them were to be sought in the analysis itself.

Lebowitz's article includes a proposition that is without foundation but widely accepted nevertheless. He maintains that Sraffa's prices of production are identical to those that would be ascribed to products in a socialist economy in which development was planned. And: 'To demonstrate the good fit of the Sraffa model to a distinct

---

[47] In *Science and Society*, no. 4, 1973-4.
[48] Ibid., p. 389.

social system is to underscore its inappropriateness as a representation of capitalism.'[49] It is probable that Lebowitz is alluding to the implications of optimal growth theory. Let us examine what this theory actually entails.

It can be assumed that a socialist economy – if one can speak in such general terms – would plan production over a given period of time, opting for the most desirable alternatives on the basis of socially established criteria of preference. In this connection there is a proposition known as the 'turnpike theorem', which may be formulated as follows. Let us say that the objective is to produce a certain package of goods, of given composition, within a specified number of time-periods, starting from given quantities of goods. Now, first consider the route that would permit the achievement of the greatest production of that particular composition; next consider the path of uniform growth at the maximum rate (the turnpike). The theorem then states that the optimal path remains close to the turnpike, except for a number of periods which depend on the proximity desired but not on the time schedule on which the plan is based.[50] In other, rather imprecise, words, the best course is to move most rapidly to the path of uniform growth, to stay on it as long as possible, and to depart from it only at the end in order to obtain the desired composition of output. If the planning schedule is reasonably short (five or ten years, for example), the number of periods spent close to the turnpike may be very small; if it is long, then uniform growth at the maximum rate prevails, but in that case the hypothesis of given technology would seem to have little sense.[51]

The turnpike theorem is paralleled by another proposition, which may be the one Lebowitz had in mind: the production techniques that would yield uniform growth at the maximum rate are those that would be chosen by capitalists, on the basis of prices entailing a uniform rate of profit and of maximization of that rate. It follows from this proposition that the prices determined by capitalist competition (uniformity and maximization of the rate of profit) should also be adopted in an efficiently planned society in order to

[49] Ibid., p. 390.

[50] R. Radner, 'Paths of Economic Growth that Are Optimal with Regard Only to Final States', in *The Review of Economic Studies*, January 1961.

[51] A. Ginzburg, 'Dal capitalismo borghese al capitalismo proletario', in *Quaderni Piacentini*, no. 44-45, 1971.

orient industry's choice of techniques. Now, according to these hypotheses, the longer the planning schedule, the more accurate this proposition becomes; for planning periods consistent with the hypothesis of given technology, however, it is not at all certain that optimal growth (with respect to the initial and final output compositions) would be close to any uniform growth path; nor is it certain that the best techniques would be those yielding the maximum rate of growth, nor, finally, that the prices that would properly orient optimal choice of technique would entail a uniform rate of profit.

A uniform rate of profit is thus a guide to efficiency *only* for planning periods long enough to make the optimal path sufficiently independent of the initial and final output compositions.[52] In general, prices of production do not coincide (even approximately) with planning prices, as should be expected since the two systems of magnitudes spring from utterly different considerations.

Several recent works utilize the analytical tools developed by Sraffa in connection with Ricardo's problem of the invariable measure to deal with Marx's transformation problem.

In several pasages of chapters 9 and 12 of *Capital* Volume 3, Marx speaks, after having expounded and discussed the transformation of values into prices, of a capital whose organic composition is equal, or approximately equal, to that of total social capital. This capital would appropriate exactly its own surplus-value, while other capitals would give or take surplus-value from other spheres of production, depending on whether their organic composition was lower or higher than average. Marx also makes use of a capital of average organic composition in chapter 11, when he examines how prices of production and the rate of profit vary with changes in distribution.[53]

On this basis some economists have supposed that Marx's central objective in the chapters on transformation was to distinguish a commodity whose characteristics were such that the rate of profit for the industry producing it, calculated on the basis of values, would be identical to the rate of profit for the system as a whole. This idea originated with Meek[54] and has recently been put forward

[52] For a balanced discussion of this topic see J. Hicks, *Capital and Growth*, Oxford, 1965, p. 235.

[53] *Capital* Volume 3, pp. 173-4, 200, 164.

[54] R. Meek, 'Mr. Sraffa's Rehabilitation of Classical Economics', in *Science and Society*, Spring 1961.

again – although in very different ways – by A. Medio and J. Eatwell. Medio[55] considers the set of industries that, directly or indirectly, produce wage-goods, and takes these industries in such proportions that total production has the same composition as the aggregate of the means of production and advances of wage-goods. In this imaginary system, the rate of profit, which is identical to that of the real system, can be calculated following Marx's method, as a ratio between total surplus-value and total capital-value (but also as a ratio between the weights of the two aggregates, since they are physically homogeneous). Eatwell, by contrast, uses the standard commodity – that is, he considers only basic commodities, in accordance with Sraffa's second definition (which does not include wage-goods unless they are basics for some other reason).[56] He then expresses wages in the standard commodity; in other words, he imagines that wages are paid in the standard commodity. On this basis he calculates the rate of surplus-value and finds that it is linearly related to the rate of profit (which, here again, is a ratio between quantities of embodied labour, relative, of course, to the imaginary system.)

The results of these studies demonstrate exactly the opposite of what they were intended to prove. They actually show that Marx's idea of compensation of differences between surplus-value and profits applies only in certain special cases; to put it another way, Marx's approach, strictly interpreted, cannot be realized. Moreover, Marx concentrates primarily on *differences* between prices and values, in explicit counterposition to Ricardo's interest in *variations*. The latter standpoint is the only important one if the primary concern is to determine the rate of profit (since prices depend on the rate of profit, which in turn is a ratio between sums of prices). It is only in this context that it makes sense to seek a commodity endowed with 'average' properties.[57] Marx's problem, however, is mainly to gauge the total labour and surplus labour reflected in prices and profits. It is therefore the rate of profit of *the real system* that

[55] A. Medio, 'Profits and Surplus-Value: Appearance and Reality in Capitalist Production, in E. Hunt and J. Schwartz (eds.), *A Critique of Economic Theory*, London, 1972.

[56] J. Eatwell, 'Value, Price and the Rate of Exploitation', duplicated text, Cambridge, 1973.

[57] Note the relevant passage from Sraffa quoted in section 2 above.

must be obtainable as a ratio between surplus-value and capital-value; Marx's definition of 'average commodity' is wholly subordinated to the idea of the redistribution of surplus-value.

When constructions like those of Medio and Eatwell are raised against Marxists who reject the consequences of Sraffa's results,[58] they merely counter the prevailing orthodoxy with a new, less rigorous variety. It consists in an attempt to sustain results achieved by isolating the *functions* of the labour theory of value in the work of the classical economists and in a search for instruments other than the labour theory of value that can fulfil them; in the meantime, a few quantities of embodied labour are grafted on and the entire endeavour is cast in Marx's terminology. What is actually required in the polemic against the 'anti-Sraffians', however, is not a new orthodoxy but a full clarification of the consequences of Sraffa's results and a decisive critique of the roots of the prevailing orthodoxy in the work of Marx.[59]

Appendix

Further on profit and surplus labour

We shall now re-examine the connection between profit and surplus labour discussed in section 3 of this chapter. Let us suppose that production for each industry is given and that there is a non-negative difference between the quantity of each commodity produced and the quantity of that commodity used as a means of production. Let us further suppose that the prices of all commodities are positive and contain positive profits (it is not necessary to assume that the rate of profit is uniform). The capitalists can therefore replace the means of production used up and purchase part of the net product. But the

---

[58] In his 'Controversies in the Theory of Surplus-Value, Old and New' (*Science and Society*, no. 3, 1975) Eatwell takes as his starting point the (orthodox) criticisms of attempts to juxtapose Sraffa and Marx presented by S. de Brunhoff, 'Marx as an A-Ricardian', *Economy and Society*, 1973. Medio's position is quite odd. Although all his work is based on the construction developed by Sraffa (with a rather unimportant variation), he believes that his interpretation can be used to criticize Sraffa from orthodox positions.

[59] On the constructs of the new orthodoxy, see Napoleoni, *Smith, Ricardo, Marx*, Turin, 1970, pp. 210-214; and Roncaglia, *Sraffa e la teoria dei prezzi*, Bari, 1975, pp. 85-86.

labour embodied in the net product is identical to the labour directly employed in the system (labour embodied in total output = labour embodied in the means of production + labour embodied in the net product = labour embodied in the means of production + labour directly employed). Thus, since profits purchase part of the net product, wages purchase commodities that embody less labour than the total contributed by the workers. The difference is surplus labour.

The same can be said even if there are some negative components of the net product (this would happen, for example, if one raw material were replaced by another because of a change in consumption.[60]) Now let us consider the aggregate of commodities bought by the workers. Imagine a system in which the net product has exactly the same composition as the aggregate of commodities purchased by the workers in the real system, and the quantity of labour directly employed is the same as in the real system. It is possible to re-proportion the real system in this manner – and thus to create a net product with no negative components – so long as the system is 'productive'; but this is also the condition for the quantities of embodied labour to be positive.[61] In our imaginary system, in which prices and wages are posited as identical to those in the real system, the proposition first demonstrated for a system in which there were no negative components of the net product remains valid. But the labour embodied in the commodities purchased with wages and the total labour expended are identical in both the real and imaginary systems.

Examination of the case in which there are negative components

---

[60] In this case too, the proposition that the labour embodied in the net product equals the labour directly employed to produce total output holds good. Let q be the row vector of total production, z the row vector of the means of production employed, y the row vector of the net product ($y = q - z$ can have negative components), m the column vector of the quantities of labour and μ the column vector of the quantities of embodied labour. We then have:

$$q\mu = (z + y)\mu = z\mu + y\mu; \quad q\mu = z\mu + qm,$$

from which it follows that $y\mu = qm$. Thus, even when the product has negative components, the labour embodied in it $(y\mu)$ – defined as the difference between the labour embodied in the surplus net products and the labour embodied in the deficit net products – equals the labour directly necessary for total production.

[61] On this point, see D. Gale, *The Theory of Linear Economic Models*, New York, 1960.

of the net product is merely a theoretical exercise. The existence of surplus labour as a precondition for the existence of profits may be seen as an obvious consequence of the fact that profits represent purchasing power over total production and of the definition of embodied labour. As we have seen in section 3 of this chapter, this proposition must not be overestimated. Neither, however, should it be underestimated, as I myself have done.[62] Marx had to deal with the confusion created by Smith's mistake, which had led to the absurd notion of profit without surplus labour. His distinction between the value added by labour-power and the value of labour-power was a fundamental step forward. In my 1974 article I expressed irritation at the superficial treatment of Marx by some economists.[63] But this does not justify the ahistorical allegation that the proposition ought to have been obvious to Marx. Nevertheless, that the proposition appears rather obvious to those equipped with the analytical tools available today, and that it was formulated against opponents long since vanquished, must be emphasized in order to combat the tendency to treat the proposition as the ultimate goal of analysis.

[62] M. Lippi, 'Lavoro produttivo, costo sociale reale e sostanza del valore nel Capitale', in *Problemi del Socialismo*, nos. 21-22, IIIrd series, 1974, pp. 330-360, and no. 1, IVth series, 1976, pp. 9-78. See p. 348.

[63] M. Morishima (*Marx's Economics*, Cambridge, 1973, p. 53) calls the proposition discussed in this appendix the 'fundamental Marxian theorem'. See also the discussion in the *Economic Journal*, with contributions from Wolfstetter ('Surplus Labour, Synchronised Labour Costs and Marx's Theory of Value', September 1973), Weizsäcker ('Morishima on Marx', December 1973), and Morishima ('Marx's Economics: A Comment on C.C. von Weizsäcker', June 1974). It is interesting to note that when the proposition on surplus labour is treated with the 'seriousness' of these articles, genuine difficulties can no longer be concealed. In the case of joint production, the quantities of embodied labour can be negative, and the same could be true of surplus-value, even though prices and the rate of profit are positive. See I. Steedman, 'Positive Profits With Negative Surplus Value', in *Economic Journal*, March 1975, and Lippi, 'Questione relative alla teoria marxiana del Capitale', in De Finetti (ed.), *Requisiti per un sistema economico accettabile in relazione alle esigenze della communità*, Milan, 1975, pp. 245-263. See also Steedman, *Marx After Sraffa*, NLB, London, 1977. I am in complete sympathy with the attempt of this book to direct the attention of Marxists to the central problems Marxism ought to be dealing with and to convince them that to do this they must discard the labour theory of value. But the importance accorded both the measure of exploitation and the 'generalized fundamental Marxian theorem' formulated by Morishima to deal with joint production (see chapter 13) is not, in my view, consistent with the spirit of the book.

V

'Capital' Without the Labour Theory of Value

1. Marx's 'Naturalism'

We know that Marx's idea of the relationship between values and prices does not lead to correct results. But we also know the source and weak point of the entire structure. Considerations about the natural background of commodity production tell us nothing about the way commodities are actually exchanged. Prices of production and quantities of embodied labour can be determined from production methods (including wages, given in terms of physical quantities). But no accurate meaning can be attributed to the proposition that prices are somehow a manifestation of values, the result of a 'transformation' of the latter. What counts is not embodied labour but the distribution in time of the quantities of labour whose sum is embodied labour.[1] There is no eternal natural law underlying the capitalist mode of production. What do exist are material elements of production which are reflected in exchange relationships, but on the basis of laws arising from the capitalist mode of production alone. It is not the case that a 'measure of difficulties' (here embodied labour) independent of the social mode of production manifests itself under capitalism; rather it is supplanted by magnitudes that reflect the need to distribute profits uniformly but that are not related to embodied labour in the simple way Marx believed. The influence on capitalist production of production in itself is far more limited than Marx thought.

On the other hand, the labour theory of value as expounded in *Capital* is an instrument with which to establish propositions about

---

[1] See section 2 of chapter 4.

the mechanisms by which capitalism functions and to refute false and potentially apologetic notions about the origin of profit. Although Marx's labour theory of value in any form that ascribes rigorous significance to the identification of value and labour is untenable, an accurate discrimination of its functions in *Capital* makes it possible to disengage these propositions and refutations from the formulation they assume in *Capital*. Fresh investigation of some of Marx's themes may thus be initiated.

The greater part of recent Marxist work on the relationship between values and prices, however, points in an opposite direction. The labour theory of value has become a bastion to be defended at all costs. At the same time, no real attempt has been made to get to the bottom of *why* Marx identified value with labour. That is why there has been no accurate distinction between the many functions of the labour theory of value in *Capital* on the one hand and the foundation of the theory itself on the other. That is also why there has been no enumeration of the objectives towards which a reconstruction of Marxist theory must strive. The result is a staggering volume of effort consisting of two sorts of projects: rather meaningless models designed to highlight quantities of embodied labour, and disjointed attacks on Sraffa and the 'neo-Ricardians'. Defences of the labour theory of value in the name of the need to delve beneath surface appearances to grasp the deeper, rational basis of reality are rarely accompanied by an understanding that Marx held that this 'basis' consisted in this proposition: behind the price of production of commodities stands value, their 'real cost'. This proposition in turn goes back to an analysis of production in general and to Marx's idea – untenable, as we now know – that a 'natural law' must necessarily assert itself in commodity production.

To be sure, it is indeed necessary to delve below surface appearances. But there is no point in continuing to attempt to do so in terms that encounter insuperable obstacles or lead to propositions devoid of meaning.[2]

[2] Even some of the best recent work on value and prices of production leads to a dead-end because of the absence of any analysis of the roots of Marx's labour theory of value, especially when facile solutions (the various 'transformations' and 'average commodities') are not accepted. On the one hand, the conclusions to which the theory of prices of production leads are fully noted; on the other, the indispensable role of the labour theory in preserving the entirety of Marx's analysis is emphasized. See, for example, Roncaglia, *Sraffa e la teoria dei prezzi*, Bari, 1975, especially chapter 7, and Benetti, *Valeur et répartition*, Paris, 1974.

2. The Movement of Capitalism

Let us extend the analysis begun in chapter 3 with an examination of how Marx links the labour theory of value to the mechanism of profit formation and the concept of capitalist exploitation. The discussion may be divided into two parts. First it must be shown that some of the central propositions of Marx's theory can be maintained without the labour theory of value. Next we can delineate the changes in the way these propositions must be viewed as a result of the abandonment of the labour theory of value.

To begin with, what is the function of the labour theory of value in formulating laws governing the phenomena of capitalist development? Everything Marx says about accumulation in chapter 25 of *Capital* Volume 1, which in a certain sense synthesizes the entire book, his analysis of the cyclical movement of accumulation as a function of the swelling and deflation of the industrial reserve army, stands or falls independent of the labour theory of value. I make no claim to have treated this point exhaustively. It is sufficient to recall that the fluctuation of the organic composition of capital, so essential in chapter 25, depends on fluctuations in the technical composition, which is the real independent variable. The organic composition rises because machines replace human workers. The labour theory of value is not indispensable here; we can refer directly to the technical composition, because everything depends on the form technological progress assumes.[3] In other words, Marx's theory can be reformulated through the theory of prices of production without any effect on its strength or weakness.[4]

The same can be said for the tendency of the rate of profit to fall. Here the significant variables are once again the organic composition (that is, in the final analysis, the technological composition) and the rate of surplus-value (that is, wages and the length of the working day). Here too it is apparent that Marx's

[3] For a treatment of the replacement of workers by machines directly in terms of prices of production, see Sylos Labini 'Technical Progress, Prices and Growth: An Introduction', duplicated text, Rome, 1975.

[4] R. Goodwin, 'A Growth Cycle', in Feinstein (ed.), *Capitalism and Economic Growth*, Cambridge, 1967, has formulated a theory of the trade cycle inspired by chapter 25 of *Capital* Volume 1.

analysis requires no reference to the labour theory of value and that its strengths and weaknesses remain unchanged.[5]

In general, there is no reason to believe that to jettison the labour theory of value is to demolish those propositions of *Capital* in which the functioning of capitalist accumulation is positively presented. On the contrary, the difficulties Marxists face in this field are wholly unconnected to the labour theory of value.

3. Commodity Fetishism

Marx's analysis of commodity fetishism is also presented in terms of the labour theory of value. Individual human labour performed by the producers independently of one another appears to them as the values of commodities. But it is clear that the considerations which this formulation expresses in terms of the theory of exchange-value (which Marx considered valid, albeit not immediately) can be formulated differently. What really counts is not so much that quantities of embodied labour, in the shape of values, seem to men to cause the movement of the things called commodities, but rather the form of the fetishism Marx discovers in the behaviour of commodity producers. The question is not whether the theory of fetishism stands or falls with the labour theory of value. The real problem is to develop Marx's suggestions about the forms fetishism assumes in the course of the history of capitalism.

The passages of *Capital* Volume 1 devoted to fetishism simply point to the general form of a relation between men in which the producers of commodities, because of their atomistic behaviour, perceive the labour expended in the production of these commodities as their objective law of motion. Now, however, we know the origin of the formulation of this argument in terms of the labour theory of value. *For reasons quite independent of the question of fetishism*, Marx holds that in the final analysis the theory of value has to do only with quantities of embodied labour. It is obvious that in the treatment of the relation between men and things which is fetishism, human labour alone figures on one side

---

[5] See B. Schefold, 'Capitale fisso, accumulazione e progresso tecnico', in *Contributi alla teoria della produzione congiunta*, Bologna, 1978.

of the relation. But this is only because of an autonomous elaboration of value.

Once the difficulties of the labour theory of value have been discovered, however, we know that the laws that stand outside the control of the producers – and appear to them as natural laws – cannot be traced back to quantities of labour. The reality is more complex: quantities of labour are bound up with the necessary uniformity of the rate of profit such that taken in itself the labour embodied in commodities is no longer a significant magnitude. What appears to the producers in the form of exchange-value cannot be reduced simply to the 'measurement of the obstacles' encountered in the production of commodities; it is rather a matter of magnitudes that have lost all 'natural' significance. But this does not demolish Marx's theory of fetishism. On the contrary, the historical dimension of capitalist production is even more strongly emphasized. The exchange-values of commodities do not express meaningful magnitudes outside the context of capitalism.

The real problem lies elsewhere. Once again, lack of interest in the reasons for the labour theory of value is reflected in an inability to distinguish Marx's formulation, obviously cast in terms of the labour theory of value, from the general form of fetishism he discovered, the result being the complete stagnation of the theory. The real problems lie in finance capital, monetary institutions, the great concentrations of capital, trade-unions, and so on, which are the subjects of fetishism. There is no point in continuing to discuss at the highly generalized level of 'independent private producers'.

The theory of fetishism is the highest point of the 'critique of political economy'. The scientific structure that culminates in Ricardo's *Principles* is assumed to reflect *truly* the laws of motion of the capitalist system; nevertheless, Marx argued, it remains limited to the viewpoint of this mode of production. Although it advances an image that conforms to its object, it fixes that object as the mode of production in general. The result is that what is actually valid only for commodity production appears to political economy 'to be just as ultimately valid as the fact that the scientific dissection of the air into its component parts left the atmosphere itself unaltered in its physical configuration'.[6]

[6] *Capital* Volume 1, p. 167.

As we have seen, this critique concerns primarily Ricardo and the best aspects of Smith.[7] It should not be confused with Marx's critique of Malthus, for example, or of the Smith who upheld the 'addition' theory of value, or of the outright degeneration of the classical school into 'vulgar economy'. Such cases involve not fetishism accompanied by 'true' propositions, but *mystifications*, entanglements in mere surface appearances. In this respect, Marx continues the work of Ricardo.[8]

It is important to emphasize that Sraffa's *Production of Commodities by Means of Commodities* is conceived in these sorts of terms. The diffidence of so many Marxists towards Sraffa probably results in part from confusion about this point. They have not understood that the object of Marx's theory of fetishism is a theoretical representation he considered correct but criticized as such. As we have tried to show, this object must be subjected to substantial modifications, although this does not rule out the possibility of criticizing it along the lines indicated by Marx.[9]

4. The Anarchy of Commodity Production

I have argued that the functions of the labour theory of value in various sections of Marx's analysis can be separated from the theory as such and that many of Marx's propositions can be reformulated. The list of such propositions could be extended, and paralleled by a second list of those that must be jettisoned. But such an exercise would be of little interest unless it was preceded by an attempt to clarify the consequences of the abandonment of the labour theory

[7] See, for example, *Capital* Volume 1, p. 174n, where, following the statement that political economy 'has indeed analysed value and its magnitude however incompletely', Marx refers to Smith and Ricardo as the 'best representatives' of classical political economy.

[8] In this connection, note the opening chapters of *Capital* Volume 3 and, of course, *Theories of Surplus-Value*.

[9] Marginal theory has long been regarded by Marxists as an extension of vulgar economics, an *immediate* representation of the interests of the ruling classes (it is sufficient to recall Bukharin's *The Economic Theory of the Leisure Class*). We shall not dwell on the validity of this view. Let us recall, however, that important conclusions were drawn by fighting on terrain similar to that on which Ricardo and Marx confronted Smith, Malthus, and Torrens (see chapter 4, note 36 of this book).

of value for the definition of the limitations and objectives of Marxism as a science.

The idea that underlies the labour theory of value has already been analysed. For Marx, social production in general is the distribution of total social labour among the members of society. Labour differentiates man from other natural beings; labour is the capacity to act consciously and collectively within the limits of the laws of nature and thus – within these limits – labour is freedom. The things that are produced are, in general, none other than this labour embodied in objects. This and this alone belongs to the essence of associated human life.

On the other hand, there are the particular forms in which associated human life is expressed. These can be classified according to the position labour occupies in them. Communism represents a form of social organization that corresponds completely to that essence, a synthesis of the primitive unity of mankind and the complete development of the productive forces. Capitalist society, as Marx sees it, stands in a twofold relation to the essence of associated human life, for it is simultaneously its manifestation and negation. It is a manifestation because behind the historically determined form stand the laws of production in general. It is a negation because these laws of social production operate in a highly asocial context. Now – and this is the whole point – this approach becomes *science*, in Marx's view, through the *demonstration* that the laws of commodity production are subordinate to the laws of production in general, and the whole burden of proof rests upon the labour theory of value. If it is true that products are nothing but labour, then we must discover this labour beneath the surface appearance of commodity production. Whatever the form in which value appears – be it price of production, circulation cost, money – it must be traced back to labour. If this task is successfully completed, if it can be shown that contrary to appearances labour is the sole source of value, then labour is *confirmed* as the essence of production. The goal of communism, as the overcoming of the alienation labour suffers under capitalism, is thereby legitimized. (This argument, of course, could be developed well beyond these brief concluding notes. It would be particularly necessary to uncover the connection between these aspects of the foundations of *Capital* and the traces in Marx of a theory that the collapse of capitalism is inevitable).

Marx's proposition that labour as real social cost is value is accompanied by his assertion that the task of science is to verify that all the rest consists only of the *forms* in which value, and therefore labour, is manifested.[10] If prices of production cannot be traced back to values and thus to labour, then we are faced with more than the mere recasting of a theory consistent with the uniformity of the rate of profit, for such a task can be accomplished only after reconsideration of the entire structure.

Now, where does Marxism stand with respect to all this? To begin with, the untenability of the labour theory of value does not spring from the discovery of an alternative source of value. On the contrary, prices of production express only the condition of the uniformity of the rate of profit and nothing more. One of the tasks Marx ascribed to the theory of value − to show that the notion that capital produced value was an illusion – has been largely accomplished, and Marx's intuition partially confirmed. Marx believed this could be done only 'positively', by tracing prices back to labour. We now know that it can be done by considering prices alone.

Thus, while the aspect of Marx's theory that states that commodity production must be shown to be a manifestation of the essence of production in general must be abandoned, there is a complementary aspect that can be fully recovered. In it commodity production is presented as the very antithesis of associated human life, a fragmentation unprecedented in history. This is why, Marx's theory holds, the labour that produces commodities appears as value and not as a conscious measure of production.

The pre-eminent place in Marx's theory of the real oppositions of capitalist society is a consequence of this second aspect of the relationship between commodity production and production in general. It is this aspect that must be grasped and maintained. Marx was alone among 'economists' in placing crisis at the centre of his portrayal of capitalist society, exactly because he considered that society both manifestation and negation of production in general. In other words, the prominence of the anarchic aspects of capitalism in Marx's thought is rooted in the idea that the essence of human social life is not atomized individual decisions devoid of coordination.

---

[10] Recall the definition of the task of science in Marx's letter to Kugelmann.

Those familiar with Marx may consider this idea a platitude. But to understand why it could be the foundation of a new science striving to transcend its own object, it is only necessary to contrast it to the predominant economic thought of the latter half of the nineteenth century, and even to that of the classical economists.

Let us look again at these two aspects of the relationship between commodity production and production in general. The first aspect entails the attempt to prove that value is a manifestation of labour, which is therefore confirmed as the sole active source of production. This aspect must be abandoned. Some important results, however, directly or indirectly rooted in the works of Marx and Ricardo, do remain, achieved through the critique of the idea that capital is a source of value, both in the form in which this idea assumed in Marx's time and in that assumed in marginalism. Marx's objective has been achieved, albeit only by refuting what it was intended to negate.[11]

Although the positive aspect of Marx's view of the relationship between commodity production and production in general collapses, the concept that capitalism is the very antithesis of social production must remain the central one of the investigation. In this context we can return to Marx's theory – particularly those aspects of it that arise from the general idea of the anarchy of commodity production, such as the theory of money and of crisis – and continue the process of disengaging it from the labour theory of value.

5. Teleology in Historical Materialism

We must now note, however, that the abandonment of the labour theory of value does entail a fundamental divergence from Marx. Reference to social production in general remains the linchpin of Marxist scientific argumentation. Social production in general, however, is an ideal concept the manifestations of which cannot be found, or demonstrated, in commodity production.

[11] It is important to emphasize that the idea that capital is 'productive of value', which was the target of Marx's attack, must not be confused with the 'productivity of capital' of the marginalists (see section 3 of chapter 4). Here we are implicitly establishing a continuity between Marx and the writers who have made the greatest contributions to the critique of marginalism.

If Marxism begins from the anarchy of capitalist production, this is surely because it views the present mode of production in opposition to production in general. The latter, however, is not an entity endowed with its own laws making it evident, but only an end to which knowledge is orientated. Marxism as science is characterized by its focus, within the capitalist totality, on the real oppositions of that totality. It then develops as the theory that these oppositions cannot be extirpated. 'Bourgeois' economics, by contrast, assumes the compatibility of the forces at work within commodity production; it then develops as the theory of harmony and welfare.[12]

With this in mind, let us return again to the problem of fetishism. When I asserted that Marx's approach to this question could be conserved regardless of the validity of the labour theory of value, I was inflecting that approach in the light of these last considerations. The inversion that is fetishism for Marx is an inversion with respect to an essence so real as to dominate commodity production, in the form of the law of value. From my point of view, too, there is an inversion, but with respect to an idea: that if production were organized consciously, the products of labour could be shorn of their form as commodities. Naturally, this idea has its real foundation in the history of capitalism and the real movement for communism; but no science could possibly show it to be necessary.

But this does not mean that Marxism is reduced to a utopia. On the contrary, the centrality it ascribes to the divergences of capitalist production from consciously organized production is an extremely rich source of positive scientific progress. The critique of Say's Law, which for Marx was an almost immediate consequence of the lack of co-ordination of individual decisions on which the concept of capitalist anarchy was based, was incorporated into marginalist theory only with great difficulty − after the shock of the crash of

---

[12] Here, of course, we are referring to the attempt to demonstrate that the equilibrium of supply and demand (of products and of 'factors' of production) leads to a situation of full and optimal use of available resources, including full employment of the work force. We are, however, excluding Keynes's *General Theory* and some of the developments to which it has given rise. The theoretical origins of Keynes's work lie in marginalism, and Keynes himself explicitly favoured preservation of the existing social order. But his work contains ideas and analytical tools which, regardless of their form of presentation in the *General Theory*, originate in direct perception of some of the causes of capitalist crises.

1929. In this sense – as a theory whose object of study is capitalism and which, in order to understand it begins by recognizing that it is different from and opposite to planned production – Marxism is scientific socialism.[13]

This whole argument represents a significant divergence from what Marxists generally mean by 'science'. We have become accustomed to exclude finalistic elements from theoretical discourse, an attitude very much in the tradition of Marx's own thought. Certainly I do not expect to inflect such an outlook with these brief concluding notes. But if the analysis of the theory of value that has been presented here leads to reflection on the state of Marxism as a science, that result alone will be gratifying.

[13] It is perhaps advisable to emphasize that propositions like that which demonstrates that profits are impossible without surplus labour are of little help here. They cannot form the basis of scientific progress because they exhaust their objective in themselves. To say that capitalist production is anarchic is to establish its divergence from a harmonious vision and therefore to utter an 'ideological' characterization. But the strength of this proposition lies in the extremely fruitful way it orients the investigation of money, for example. This 'non-neutral' assertion thus becomes the source of other, more precise propositions. Similarly, to say that the precondition for the existence of profit under commodity production is the reduction of labour-power to a commodity, is to formulate an instrument of historical analysis. But to say that if there are to be profits the workers must work more than is needed to reconstitute their wages does not produce anything in the way of scientific construction. It is a teleological proposition, since the stress is on labour. But it is only that and offers no possibility of development. (On the role of this proposition in Marx's work, see section 3 of chapter 4.)

Postscript

There is a passage in *Capital* Volume 3 that demonstrates with particular clarity my argument about the basis of the identity of labour and value as Marx conceived it. He writes: 'Although the form of labour as wage-labour is decisive for the form of the entire process and the specific mode of production itself, it is not wage-labour which determines value. In the determination of value, it is a question of social labour-time in general, the quantity of labour which society generally has at its disposal, as it were, their respective social importance. The definite form in which the social labour-time prevails as decisive in the determination of the value of commodities is of course connected with the form of labour as wage-labour and with the corresponding form of the means of production as capital, in so far as solely on this basis does commodity-production become the general form of production'.[1]

Here, as elsewhere in Marx's work, we find a distinction between 'social labour-time in general' and 'the form' it assumes when labour is paid wages, in other words, when production is capitalist commodity production. Moreover, the explicit admonition that the basis of the identity of value and labour must be established *prior to* consideration of the form social labour-time assumes under commodity production is formulated so as to rule out any possible misunderstanding: the value *form* assumed by the labour embodied in products depends on the *form* of labour as counterposed to capital, or wage-labour. The *content*, however, is the 'relative

[1] *Capital* Volume 3, p. 882. This passage, which had always escaped me, was mentioned by S. Veca in his recent *Saggio sul programma scientifico di Marx* (Milan 1977). This work, especially chapter 4, provided the initial impetus for much of what follows here.

absorption' of social labour-time, which *in general* determines the 'social weight' of each product; under commodity production this weight assumes the form of value.

The formulation here is quite similar to that stated explicitly in the famous letter to Kugelmann of 11 July 1868 and implicitly elsewhere in Marx's work: value is the form assumed by the measurement of products in labour-time under capitalism. Whatever the mode of production, 'products *are* labour';[2] When products are commodities, their being nothing but labour is 'hidden' behind exchange relations. Political economy, Marx argues, has been able to discover, albeit incompletely, that it is labour that is manifested in those relations; but it has not managed to conceive the labour-time contained in products otherwise than as the value form, or, what amounts to the same thing, it has not succeeded in distinguishing between production in general and commodity production.

I should like to comment on the 'genealogy' of this reconstruction of Marx's thought. It has been claimed that I have merely repeated an argument that has already been advanced by others.[3] This is certainly true, as I myself have explicitly pointed out; indeed, most Marxist literature refers to some general principle to justify the identification of value and labour.[4] On the other hand, it seems to me that there is no need even to ask whether my interpretation is orginal, since Marx himself clearly stated the basis of his identification of value and labour; it is not a matter of extrapolating an idea somehow concealed in the text, for the 'project' is set out transparently and completely.

For my part, I have merely attempted to show how consistently the general concept of labour as 'real social cost' is developed in *Capital* and elsewhere; then, since I hold that this idea leads to unacceptable conclusions, I have maintained that the *functions* of the labour theory of value in Marx's construction of a *theory of capitalism* must be separated from the theory as such. I shall return to this later; for the moment I would only stress that my reconstruction of Marx's theory of value is aimed above all at

---

[2] *Grundrisse*, p. 613. This brief quotation is taken from pages from which I quote extensively in section 6 of chapter 1 above.

[3] See the articles by C. Napoleoni, *Rinascità*, no. 13, 1977, and R. Racinaro, in *Critica Marxista*, no. 1, 1977.

[4] See above, chapter 2, section 4, as well as my article in *Rinascita*, no. 18, 1977.

highlighting a point which is quite explicit in Marx and has been either completely forgotten or uncritically taken for granted by Marxist thought.

At the root of Marx's labour theory of value, then, lies the idea that the measurement of products in labour must be manifested under commodity production; there is nothing particularly capitalist about this measurement, which simply ascribes to products their real cost to society, which must be done under any mode of production. The characteristic of capitalism here is only the way this measurement is asserted, since it remains hidden in the wings, so to speak, a twofold mediation being required to reach observable magnitudes.[5]

This still seems to me to be a fair statement of Marx's ideas; it may, however, be appropriate to return to the general notion of 'measurement in labour', and to this end, to examine carefully various passages in which Marx 'differentiates' the capitalist mode of production from others past or possible in the future. I will thus be able to develop and clarify my argument.

Let us look first at three passages in which commodity production is compared with different modes of production: the analysis of the commodity in *A Contribution to the Critique of Political Economy*, the section on 'Fetishism of the Commodity and its Secret' in the first chapter of *Capital* Volume 1, and the *Critique of the Gotha Programme*.

In *Capital* Marx cites four examples: 'Robinson Crusoe on his island', the *corvée* of the serf in medieval Europe, 'the patriarchal rural industry of a peasant family', and 'an association of free men'. The second and third examples had been previously employed in *A Contribution to the Critique of Political Economy*, while the first and the fourth appear only in *Capital*. The fourth is then developed in the *Critique of the Gotha Programme*, 'the co-operative society' that would follow capitalism.

Consider first the examples common to *Capital* and the *Critique of Political Economy*. They are used to identify this characteristic

---

[5] 'Observable magnitudes' means market prices. As Marx sees it, these 'gravitate' towards prices of production which are in turn obtained from values through a process of 'transformation'.

of commodity production, that in such a system individual labour becomes social in the form of abstract universality, which is unlike the other modes of production, in which the 'natural form of labour, its particularity...is here its immediate social form'.[6] In other words, the reduction of the various useful tasks performed by various individuals to homogeneous labour, to the pure 'expenditure of *human* brains, muscles, nerves, hands', etc.,[7] distinguishes commodity production from prior modes of production, in which the various functions of society were assigned to individuals chosen according to age, sex, etc. and the labours of these individuals were immediately social in their particularity.

Two points must be made here. First, this reduction forms the foundation of a measurement in labour in the strict sense, namely the attribution to products of a *quantity* of embodied labour. In other words, a genuine measurement in labour occurs only under commodity production, at least of the instances considered so far. Nevertheless – and this is the second point – while it is not a feature of every mode of production, the reduction to homogeneous labour rests on solid natural foundations: 'The mystical character of the commodity does not therefore arise from its use-value. Just as little does it proceed from the nature of the determinants *of value*. For in the first place, however varied the useful kinds of labour, or productive activities, it is a *physiological* fact that they are functions of the *human* organism, and that each such function, whatever may be its nature or its form, is essentially the expenditure of *human* brain, nerves, muscles, and sense organs. Secondly, with regard to the foundation of the quantitative determination of value, namely the *duration* of that expenditure or the *quantity* of labour, this is quite palpably different from its quality. In all situations, the *labour-time* it costs to produce the means of subsistence must necessarily concern mankind, although not to the same degree at different stages of development. And finally, as soon as men start to work for each other in any way, their labour also assumes a social form.'[8]

Thus, the reduction to homogeneous labour that occurs under

[6] *Capital* Volume 1, p. 170. For an almost identical proposition based on the same example see *Contribution to the Critique of Political Economy*, p. 33.

[7] *Capital* Volume 1, p. 134 (emphasis added).

[8] Ibid., p. 164 (emphasis added).

commodity production for the first time is not at all 'enigmatic'; the various types of useful work are so many instances of the capacity – defined in terms of functions: brain, muscles, etc. – to act consciously towards one or another end. The equalization of various human labours, while it *distinguishes* commodity production from previous modes of production and is the precondition for the constitution of the magnitude of value, is nevertheless a *natural* potential; moreover, it is not sufficient to define commodity production completely.

Marx arrives at this definition as follows, in a passage subsequent to the one just cited: 'Men do not therefore bring the products of their labour into relation with each other as values because they see these objects merely as the *material integuments* of homogeneous human labour. The reverse is true: by *equating* their different *products* to each other in exchange *as values*, they equate their different kinds of labour as human labour. They do this without being aware of it.'[9] The central characteristic of capitalism, then, lies not so much in the reduction to homogeneous labour – although this is a feature in it alone – as in the way labour and its magnitude 'adhere to' products, in the 'objectivity' of value.

His identification of the 'fetishism of the commodity' enabled Marx to sharpen the difference between capitalism and previous modes of production on the one hand and the future 'association of free men' or 'collectivist society' on the other. The latter, Marx held, would measure products in labour just like commodity production, and therefore would also equalize human labour in the same manner, the equalization being a precondition of the measurement; but this measurement would occur as the conscious attribution of a particular social weight to products, and not, as under capitalism, as a law operating behind the backs of the producers.[10]

Let us try to summarize the argument thus far. There is no doubt

[9] Ibid., pp. 166-167 (emphasis added).

[10] There is a shift in emphasis as Marx moves from the *Contribution* to *Capital* to the introduction of the 'association of free men' as one of the modes of production from which capitalism must be distinguished. In the *Contribution*, Marx lays considerable stress on the reduction to homogeneous labour, while the 'fetishism of the commodity' is given slight attention at the end of the discussion; in *Capital* it is the other way round.

that Marx holds that one can speak of a measurement in labour, understood as a genuine quantity, only under commodity production and the 'collectivist society' that succeeds it (under which the material conditions are established for the advent of a communist society in which a measurement in labour is no longer needed). This measure, however, is presented as the manifestation of a natural foundation, while the distinguishing feature of commodity production, particularly with respect to the co-operative society with which it has in common the reduction to homogeneous labour, lies in the way in which the 'natural' magnitudes are asserted – even though they are not common to every mode of production. Such are the terms of comparison Marx uses in distinguishing commodity production from other modes of production.

Now, if we bear in mind what has been said about pre-capitalist social formations, Marx's use of abstractions like 'measurement in labour' in reference to production *in general* seems to conflict with formulations in which reduction to homogeneous labour is cited as characteristic only of some modes of production. This is the question that I wanted to pose in regard to my reconstruction, in which I attribute to Marx the idea that value is only the form assumed under capitalism by a magnitude valid for all modes of production. This thesis, I would hold, can be substantiated, but certain points barely touched upon in my essay must be developed fully.

The terms of the problem must be carefully defined. In some passages, such as the letter to Kugelmann, Marx presents the law of value as valid in general; elsewhere, in the *Grundrisse*, for example, there are assertions like: 'only because products ARE labour can they be measured by the measure of labour, by labour time, the amount of labour consumed in them',[11] in which the reference is to production in itself, regardless of its particular historical and social form; finally, there are passages in which the very constitution of a magnitude of embodied labour is unequivocally described as a feature of commodity production. What is the relationship among these various treatments?

[11] *Grundrisse*, p. 613.

In my opinion there can be no talk of two contradictory yet coexistent lines of thought in Marx's work. If such were the case, it should be possible to distinguish periods or groups of writings; in fact, however, the two lines are found together in every period and every text. It would therefore seem more useful to attempt a convincing explanation of their coexistence.

To begin with, Marx's abstractions like 'measurement in labour' or 'law of nature' in reference to production in general must not be viewed as concepts subsuming unrelated objects. The modes of production to which these abstractions refer are *ordered* within a process of development: 'Bourgeois society is the most developed and the most complex historic organization of production. The categories which express its relations, the comprehension of its structure, thereby also allows insights into the structure and the relations of production of all the vanished social formations out of whose ruins and elements it built itself up, whose partly still unconquered remnants are carried along within it, whose mere nuances have developed explicit significance within it, etc. Human anatomy contains a key to the anatomy of the ape. The intimations of higher development among the subordinate animal species, however, can be understood only after the higher development is already known. The bourgeois economy thus supplies the key to the ancient, etc. But not at all in the manner of those economists who smudge over all historical differences and see bourgeois relations in all forms of society.'[12] From ape to man − we are thus dealing with the necessary transition from lower to higher forms. It is not a matter of mere *differences* between modes of production advanced to determine the characteristics of capitalism, but of differences *directed* from the simple to the complex.

Marx also considers labour in 'bourgeois society' as a more developed form of labour in pre-capitalist societies and counterposed to it as such: 'Indifference towards specific labours corresponds to a form of society in which individuals can with ease transfer from one labour to another, and where the specific kind is a matter of chance for them, hence of indifference. Not only the category, labour, but labour in reality has here become the means of creating wealth in general, and has ceased to be organically linked

---

[12] Introduction of 1857 to the *Grundrisse*, in *Grundrisse*, p. 105.

with particular individuals in any specific form.'[13] Here there are two important themes: on the one hand, the element of 'progress', represented by the rupture under commodity production of the bond between individual and particular useful activity; on the other hand, the 'generic quality' that labour thereby acquires takes the form of 'indifference' to the content of labour. In sum, labour becomes generic simultaneous with its estrangement from the worker who performs it.[14]

I shall not dwell on this point. My intention is only to recall that the process of development from lower to higher forms serves as a backdrop for Marx's whole construction.[15] With this idea in mind it

[13] Ibid., p. 104.

[14] Marx refers to human labour as generic activity in two different but connected senses. The first is that implicit in the passage from *Capital* cited above, in which the variety of useful activities are seen as manifestations of a generic capacity for work, described as a 'physiological' reality. In this sense human labour is always generic, even when the social mode of production is such that the individual activities seem to adhere 'naturally' to certain particular groups and individuals. Under commodity production, the consideration of the various useful tasks as the expression of human labour in general, which is the foundation of exchange-value, ceases to be a purely physiological reality and becomes the basis of economic life. Generic labour no longer refers to the species as a whole but to every individual worker. This occurs, however, not by virtue of the positive universality of each individual, but because all the particular useful labours are emptied of content. This is the special form assumed by the genericness of human labour under capitalism. This, I believe, is an area of Marx's thought that is difficult to understand properly without acknowledging 'contradiction' (although I am not saying that it is impossible to reformulate the argument so as to avoid it). Indeed, Marx maintains that the universality of labour is both realized and negated in wage-labour. It is the universality not of 'being able to do everything' but of 'not being able to do anything', since the capacity of the worker is transferred to means of production that are estranged from him, just as the science that conceived these means of production is estranged from him. These observations, however, are not directly related to the question of Marx's foundation of value which we are considering here; what is important here is the possibility of measuring *cost in labour*, and therefore the reduction to homogeneous quantities of generic human labour, regardless of how it comes about. On this point, see also the passage of *Capital* Volume 3 quoted at the beginning of this Postscript and the distinction it makes between labour in general and the form it assumes under commodity production.

[15] It is perhaps apposite to recall one famous passage in which the stages of this process are explicitly enumerated: 'In broad outlines asiatic, ancient, feudal, and modern bourgeois modes of production can be designated as progressive epochs in the economic formation of society. The bourgeois relations of production are the last antagonistic form of the social process of production...; at the same time the productive forces developing in the womb of bourgeois society create the material conditions for the solution of that antagonism. This social formation brings, therefore, the prehistory of human society to a close.' (Preface to *A Contribution to*

seems to me easier to understand Marx's use of abstractions like 'measurement in labour'. Sometimes these refer to features of the more 'complex' forms of development and are pertinent to them alone; at other times, they refer without distinction to all phases of the process, to the higher stages in the strict sense, but to the lower in that these contain them only potentially, barely noticeably, and not yet 'developed in all its significance'.[16]

Genuine measurement in labour thus belongs to the higher stages of development: to commodity production and co-operative society. Here too, however, there is a directed distinction. It is my view that Marx held that measurement of labour in its pure form is characteristic only of co-operative society.

Let me clarify this point. At first sight, co-operative society may appear to be an *ad hoc* construction designed to identify the characteristics of capitalism. Again at first sight, it is none other than commodity production deprived of certain of its features, such as the anarchy of production, class divisions, and so on. And this is probably true — but only as regards the genesis of the idea, or of that of the 'law of nature', in Marx's thought. But if we think of Marx's presentation of such ideas as mirroring a real state of affairs, then things look very different. *First* comes the general law, the 'rational' and 'necessary' rule for attributing a 'social weight' to products. In the co-operative society this law is asserted consciously and immediately, together with the operations on which the measurement in labour is based: average necessary labour-time and reduction to simple labour on the basis of the time required to train complex labour-power.[17] Value in labour, *as a magnitude*, is precisely the measurement in labour under the co-operative society. I have laid great stress upon this point, on the derivation of the magnitude of value from considerations 'external' to the problem of the theoretical representation of commodity production as such: the

the Critique of Political Economy, 1857, from *Marx-Engels: Selected Works*, Volume I, Moscow, 1951 p. 329.)

[16] As an example of this second manner of use of these abstractions, see the passage from the section of *Capital* on 'commodity fetishism' in which measurement in labour refers to production in general. See also the note to this passage, where mention is made of the 'ancient Germans', who measured land according to the labour of a day.

[17] *Critique of the Gotha Programme*, in *Marx-Engels: Selected Works*, Volume II, Moscow, 1958, p. 22-3.

exclusion from value of costs that arise solely from the commodity form of the product; the predominance of the logic of real cost in the determination of 'market-value' as average value, whereas the really decisive factor is the structure of industries in which varying methods of production coexist. (In this connection see also the qualification of the market-value of agricultural production, calculated on the less fertile lands, as 'false social value', the 'real' value being that calculated on average lands.[18])

The measure in labour of co-operative society is thus the *prius* of labour-value; according to Marx, it is not obtained as an abstraction from commodity production; rather labour-value is its specification, one of its 'forms'. The general law, acting through values and their transformation into prices, regulates commodity production, but only as an average of market fluctuations: 'The point of bourgeois society consists precisely in this, that *a priori* there is no conscious, social regulation of production. The rational and naturally necessary asserts itself only as a blindly working average.'[19]

Let us now return to the problem raised at the beginning of this section. Marx's general law has one principal paradigm: the co-operative society mentioned in *Capital* and the *Critique of the Gotha Programme*. The law that regulates the ultimate situation[20] – namely the measurement of products by the quantities of labour required to obtain them – also prevails, *in specific forms and at varying degrees of maturity*, in the intermediate stages of the process. It is a matter, then – and this is a point on which my book is insufficiently explicit and even somewhat dubious at times – of a general law, but in a special sense: it is not that all modes of production *actually* conform to the law; rather, it is the central characteristic of the society towards which the historical process that embodies these modes of production is evolving.

In other words, the law of value is described as the form the general law assumes under commodity production; but the general

---

[18] See chapter 1 above.
[19] 'Letter to Kugelmann, 11 July 1868', in *Marx-Engels: Selected Works*, Volume II, Moscow, 1958, pp. 461-2.
[20] 'Ultimate' refers only to that period of history which Marx describes as dominated by the need to measure products in labour. This phase, Marx held, would be followed by one in which such a measure would no longer be needed.

law cannot be merely what all modes of production have in common, since such an abstraction would be too feeble to permit understanding of such a complex social formation as capitalism, as Marx was well aware, for he knew that measurement in labour in the strict sense was possible only under historical and social conditions that would permit the equalization of varying individual labours. A law 'common' to all modes of production would therefore have no quantitative content, but would amount merely to the general attribution to each product of the particular inputs required to obtain it. But then the general law, asserted under commodity production as the law of value, if it is to be sufficiently rich to be of use in explaining the whole gamut of successive modes of production, *including* commodity production, must be drawn from a phase of this process subsequent to all others and in this sense the most general of all. This phase is precisely the consciously organized production of co-operative society.[21]

Let us now attempt to reformulate the problem critically.

The labour theory of value has two functions in Marx's theoretical construction. It is used in the investigation of a strictly analytical problem relating to commodity production, namely the determination of the general rate of profit; at the same time, it is central to the analysis of capitalism as a stage in the historical

[21] My book presents the general law as endowed with a quantitative content; moreover, I often emphasize that the operations required to effect the reduction to homogeneous labour are not specifically capitalist (having in mind particularly the 'association of free men' and 'co-operative society'). But the above observations about the ordered succession of modes of production are mentioned only fleetingly (chapter 2, section 1, pp. 20-25 and note 11). This could leave the impression that I am attributing to Marx the claim that the measurement in labour in the strict sense is proper to every mode of production. This, however, must not be confused with the proposition attributed to me by Napoleoni in his article in *Rinascità* that Marx considered value a category of production in general; this I have never maintained, nor can it be imputed to my book in any way. I would, however, like to note a passage in which, contrary to what I argue elsewhere, I do make the mistake of attributing to Marx the idea that the 'general law' is what all modes of production have in common. This occurs at the end of chapter 2, section 3, where I erroneously link a proposition of the 1857 introduction and the letter to Kugelmann. (On this point see the review by G. Conte in *Il Manifesto*, 24 April 1977.) On the other hand, I would still maintain my assertions about Marx's 'naturalism' in those same passages, for this consists in the untenable attempt to deduce the law of value from observations about production in general, even though production in general must not be understood in the vulgar sense.

process. It is my view that Marx's conviction that he had solved the problem of the rate of profit through the labour theory of value reinforced his adherence to the general idea that labour was the real cost of products, which was common to the two areas of research. But I also believe that it is not possible fully to understand Marx's analytical work without delving back to the origins of the 'project' that guided his work.

This is what I have sought to demonstrate in this book by discussing particular aspects of Marx's theory of value like the problem of circulation costs and the transformation of values into prices. The latter is dominated by the idea that it is both *necessary* and *possible* to derive prices of production from values so as to confirm the identity of value and labour (this is the origin of Marx's insistence on the *conservation* of total magnitudes of value and surplus-value).[22] The aim was not somehow to determine magnitudes that are directly observable under capitalism, but to *explain* these magnitudes as a specific instance of the operation of a general law.

This is the project, or 'task of science' as explicitly formulated by Marx. The roots of the project lie in the grafting of the labour theory of value, *as bequeathed to Marx by classical political economy*, onto the broader problematic of the 'fate' of capitalism. The content of the law, namely the measurement of products by the quantities of labour required to produce them, appeared to Marx as the rational principle of production. As such, it is the law that governs a *possible* mode of production *higher* than capitalism. But Marx did not stop at the estimation or adumbration of an end; he ascribed to 'science' the task of 'proving' that capitalism had to pass away and that the outcome of the transition would be precisely a society that could be modelled on the rational principle. The theory of crisis corresponds to the first objective; the attempt to demonstrate that the 'apparent motion' of commodity production is governed by the principle of labour as real cost to the second; even under capitalism, Marx held, despite the anarchy of the

---

[22] I have used the words 'necessary' and 'possible'. This means that when Marx set out to reduce prices of production to values and hence to labour, he believed that such a reduction could be achieved, in other words, that given the labour expended in production, prices could only be a redistribution of that labour. See chapter 3 above.

production and distribution of commodities, the same law that will regulate consciously organized production still applies.

A few last points. It does not seem to me that recognition of an implicit teleological element in Marx's scientific construction has destructive effects. Quite the contrary, I believe that much useful work can be done on the basis of an understanding of the nature of the 'tasks' Marx assigned to 'science'. Of course, certain claims about a theory of capitalism must be scaled down.[23] Rationally organized production – understood as a purely ideal construction – is undoubtedly a very important reference point in the description of the characteristics of commodity production, especially in the identification of the co-existence of regular functioning and its continuous negation, which lay at the centre of Marx's analysis. But a theory of value cannot be deduced from comparison with a system of consciously organized production. In sum, although the idea that capitalism *differs* from a society in which production is planned can be preserved, the other idea that underlies the labour theory of value – that a 'rational' general law *is manifested* under capitalism – must be abandoned.

Now, if my argument that the discussion must be shifted to analysis of the foundation of Marx's labour theory of value is accepted, then it is clear that any attempt to salvage a role for the labour theory of value through the many mathematical adjustments that have been proposed is pointless and harmful. Pointless because the 'project' embodied in the attempt to obtain prices through a 'transformation' of values can surely never be realized through a meaningless 'derivation' of prices from values;[24] harmful because defence of the labour theory of value at all costs eventually obscures the fact that Marx used this theory as an instrument for the analysis of capitalism as such, an instrument with particular *functions* in that analysis. I have tried to demonstrate that these functions can be separated from the labour theory of value and otherwise fulfilled.[25] If those of us for whom Marx provides the principle reference point

---

[23] For this point see the article by M. Salvati, 'Sul programma di ricerca sottostante alla teoria del valore marxiana', in *Quaderni Piacentini*, nos. 62-63, 1977; see also the study by Veca cited above.

[24] On this point see chapter 3 and the first section of chapter 4 above.

[25] See chapters 4 and 5 above.

strive to continue in this direction, a great step forward could be made, for it would then be realized that Marx's fundamental propositions about capitalism can be discussed, and therefore accepted or abandoned, without worrying much about the validity of the labour theory of value.

Index

This index contains no entries for Marx.

Printed and bound by CPI Group (UK) Ltd, Croydon, CR0 4YY

22/04/2026

02095406-0010